Reasoning for Business

Critical thinking skills are important in decision making, but they're not enough.

This book offers a kit of conceptual tools that empower you – an already savvy thinker – to advance your ability to reason, plan, solve problems, think abstractly, comprehend complex ideas, and learn quickly. Weaving together insights from both philosophy and psychology and more than a decade of work with professionals and leaders at all levels of businesses, government agencies, and NGOs, Haywood Spangler has written the inquirer's guide to the universe of sources offering guidance regarding civic, personal, and professional choices, from self-help books, to TED talks, to periodicals, financial planners, psychologists, and successful entrepreneurs. Rather than providing oversimplified constructs or generic answers, his book expands your perspective and thought processes, applying concepts from philosophy based on people's actual questions, needs, and challenges. It functions as a handbook, enabling the reader to consult specific chapters as needed, and as a comprehensive guide to developing personal judgment.

This book is for business leaders looking for strategies to vet the results of AI queries, human resource managers wanting to be discerning in their use of data, analysts and forecasters needing a realistic understanding of statistically based predictions – and any professional who selects tools critically to assess trends impacting their life.

Haywood Spangler, PhD, MDiv, is the founder and principal of Work & Think, LLC. He is a corporate consultant, a researcher, and an author, and was formerly a biomedical ethicist at the University of Virginia Medical Center as well as an instructor of business ethics at the University of Virginia McIntire School of Commerce.

Reasoning for Business

The Inquirer's Guide to Decision Making

Haywood Spangler

Routledge
Taylor & Francis Group

NEW YORK AND LONDON

Designed cover image: Getty

First published 2026
by Routledge
605 Third Avenue, New York, NY 10158

and by Routledge
4 Park Square, Milton Park, Abingdon, Oxon, OX14 4RN

Routledge is an imprint of the Taylor & Francis Group, an informa business

© 2026 Haywood Spangler

For Product Safety Concerns and Information please contact our EU representative GPSR@taylorandfrancis.com. Taylor & Francis Verlag GmbH, Kaufingerstraße 24, 80331 München, Germany.

ISBN: 9781041088073 (hbk)
ISBN: 9781041088066 (pbk)
ISBN: 9781003647034 (ebk)

DOI: 10.4324/9781003647034

Typeset in Sabon
by Newgen Publishing UK

For
M. V. Slusher and J. E. Cooke

Contents

Acknowledgements

I would like to thank the following professors, mentors, colleagues, friends, and family members who introduced me to the philosophical concepts in this book and who collaborated with me in developing methods for their practical application.

Marilyn McCord Adams, Robert Adams, Paul Babitts, Judy Chartrand, James Childress, Anthony Coyne, Cedric Crocker, Margaret Farley, Jamie Ferreira, Christine Giugni, Ileana Grams, Rowan Greer, Dennis Hawley, David Hopes, Daryl Howard, Charles Mathews, Nicole Morgenstern, Margaret Mohrmann, Linda Nash, Peter Ochs, Gene Outka, Gene Rogers, Abdulaziz Sachedina, Bes Spangler, John Spangler, William Spellman, Michael Thorne-Begland, Brandyn Webster, Patricia Werhane.

Chapter 1

Introduction

The Problem All Advice Seekers Face

Chapter Outline

The Problem

If you are already a well-informed thinker and savvy decision maker, what is the appeal of expert advice? At first, the answer may seem obvious. No matter how savvy you are, you recognize that you may still need the advice of an accountant who knows more than you do about tax codes. No matter how well-informed, you realize you may still need the counsel of an attorney who knows more than you do about estate planning laws. In fact, a characteristic of being a responsible professional and astute consumer is recognizing when you need to consult with others who have specialized knowledge.

Occasions of conferring with a specific experts aside, why do astute, intelligent individuals consult the plethora of sources available today: self-help books, TED talks, podcasts, and articles offered by physicians, psychologists, economists, financial planners, journalists, and successful executives, to name a few? There are multiple answers. People seek expert advice hoping to reduce uncertainty and risk. They seek informed perspectives hoping to improve their chances for personal and professional success. They seek credible insights to improve their decision making. They seek research-based best practices to feel less anxious, more confident, and happier.

DOI: 10.4324/9781003647034-1

Whilst people seek expert advice to meet these needs, the problem is that even credible, expert sources do not effectively provide what advice seekers hope for. Whether books, columns, articles, keynote talks or interviews, sources offering expert advice are often overly simplistic, falsely certain, even pushing an agenda. Rather than help people navigate uncertainty, experts may placate the desire for certainty by overpromising on the results that can be achieved with their method or insights. For example, a financial forecaster may present their claims as definitive predictions, while a popular behavioral science source may declare they have developed tools to control individuals' decision making, while giving them the illusion of choice. Similarly, rather than provide clarity, expert sources often contradict one another. News media frequently report on medical studies from equally credible institutions, but which offer contradictory findings. For instance, one study from a highly respected medical school may find that coffee promotes heart health, while another study from an equally reputable school finds that coffee is associated with heart disease. Moreover, self-help sources frequently offer tips, tricks, techniques, and purportedly foolproof solutions. These actually reinforce an advice seeker's dependence on advice, rather than facilitating advice seekers' independent thinking and decision making. While perceptive, intelligent professionals look to expert advice to help them become more astute, confident, and successful, expert advice often leads to confusion, doubt, and poorly informed, ineffective decisions. Ironically, expert advice can stymie or erode rather than enhance your sense of competence and self-confidence.

This book offers a bridge between what you – an already savvy thinker – seek and what expert advice offers. Think of this book as a decision maker's guide to the advice universe. Here, I weave together insights from both philosophy and psychology, curated through more than a decade of my work with professionals and leaders at all levels of different businesses, government agencies, and NGOs. I offer you less familiar but more sophisticated conceptual tools for navigating the sometimes murky waters of the expert advice ocean. Developed and "road tested" through my work with clients, the tools in this book will equip you to advance your ability to reason, plan, solve problems, think abstractly, critically evaluate complex ideas, and learn quickly. More importantly, the techniques will aid you in refining your own personal judgment, which is the ultimate tool for being able to self-confidently navigate life's dilemmas. This book may, paradoxically, be an "anti-self-help" self-help book, as its purpose is to aid you in developing your own thought processes and intellectual resources, rather than to offer simplistic constructs or answers.

While I approach my engagements with clients rather like an anthropologist conducting fieldwork, I should disclose that I am trained mainly in philosophy. Most consultants have a background in psychology, studying human behavior. I began my career as a university instructor of business and biomedical ethics, both of which are based on Western philosophy. I sometimes joke, "Who has ever heard of a consulting philosopher?" A consulting psychologist, yes! A consulting philosopher, not so much. My clients have appreciated the different perspective philosophy brings. You can view this book as a stealth philosophy book, written for astute thinkers, who may not yet have experienced philosophy's value.

This Book as Public Philosophy

The sociologist Robert Bellah observed that his discipline and other social sciences often view the humanities as impressionistic and anecdotal, while the methods of science produce valid knowledge. He saw an artificial boundary between social sciences and humanities that he wanted to overcome. I am sympathetic with Bellah's observation, and I offer this book as an exercise in public philosophy that engages social sciences and disciplines, such as forecasts, using scientific methods. The emerging discipline of experimental philosophy best describes my approach. I use empirical, qualitative methods to show the value and relevance of philosophical concepts for practical decision making, at the same time offering ways to assess those empirical methods.

Although philosophy has a niche in business schools in the field of business ethics, it more broadly offers clarity about thought and knowledge in ways that are distinct from other business disciplines, such as organizational psychology. Lest you be put off at this point, anticipating too much abstract speculation for practical purposes, I assure you that this is not a typical philosophy book. I did not develop the book from an "omniscient expert" perspective, judging what I think you need to know. Rather, real people's questions, real people's challenges, and, most importantly, real people's solutions have determined the philosophical concepts I share in these pages.[1]

How This Book Benefits You

This book presents advanced critical thinking techniques. Like the clients I have been privileged to work with, you are probably already familiar with what I sometimes refer to as "Critical Thinking 101," which includes skills such as recognizing weak arguments, understanding cognitive biases, identifying false inferences, and detecting spurious correlations. Such critical thinking skills are crucial in everyone's professional and personal lives today. These skills allow you, for instance, to distinguish fact from opinion on social media. These foundational skills are not, however, sufficient to help you assess the accuracy of a financial forecast or the completeness and relevance of healthcare information. Recognizing rhetoric and cognitive biases does not in itself help you to adjudicate conflicting findings from equally credible experts, or detect when a financial planner may be overpromising your security in the future.

Realistically assessing expert perspectives, and determining their relevance for you, thus requires more nuanced techniques. Without these more refined techniques, it is easy to mistake an expert's hypothesis based on observation or statistical testing as a definitive conclusion about some aspect of reality. Such mistakes can lead even self-reflective, reasonable people to make poorly informed choices regarding significant life issues, ranging from major purchases, to philanthropy, to parenting, to caring for aging parents. The techniques and methods offered here will enable you to assess critically trends impacting your life. They will equip you to vet better the results of artificial intelligence (AI) queries and anticipate how best to leverage AI as a tool for your work. The methods presented in the following chapters will allow you to be discerning in the application of human resources (HR) "science" in your professional roles. They will provide you with a more realistic understanding of statistically based predictions when you use forecasts as part of your job and in your personal life, such as when you purchase a home or plan for retirement. They can help you achieve a more subtle, accurate understanding of data used in public policy decisions. If you pursue community leadership positions as part of your civic life, these tools will help you distill data more effectively for public policy making.

The techniques described in the following chapters may not filter *all* the white noise transmitted throughout the advice universe, but they will allow you to do the following:

- Determine how different claims and assertions in public discourse are true.
- Recognize the underlying logic of different types of forecasts.
- Realistically assess predictions based on forecasts.
- Understand where and how scientific methods are most usefully applied.
- Accurately assess recommendations presented as based on science.
- Effectively navigate circumstances – dilemmas – in which no specific expert recommendation provides a solution.

- Build trust in your own personal judgment as your guide for complex, crucial life decisions.

While this book is compact, it draws on years of work figuring out which advanced reasoning techniques matter most. The work of a consultant is often like the work of an anthropologist who is a participant observer. Anthropologists immerse themselves in a social group, simultaneously participating in activities and documenting behaviors and practices. Likewise, I have immersed myself in the work of my clients, both helping them and documenting what we have learned together. Consequently, I view my work with clients as a kind of fieldwork. If I understand my practice as fieldwork resulting in qualitative research, then I can say that the tools and methods offered in this book have been developed in the laboratory of real life. As a participant observer, I have collaborated with a diverse array of professionals in organizations ranging from finance and financial technology, to biotechnology, to military intelligence, to manufacturing, to the arts and cultural institutions.

I have consulted with individuals in these organizations as thought partner, coach, facilitator, seminar leader, and, often, friend. As a thought partner, I have counseled clients as they interpreted recommendations from financial planners and marketing experts. As a coach, I have listened and offered Socratic questions as clients sought to apply insights from behavioral science to their management practice and their personal relationships. Likewise, I have offered analysis as clients sought credible information and answers from their trusted news media sources. What I learned through this fieldwork was the expert sources that savvy professionals consult most often. For this book, I have organized the expert sources into three categories:

- **Public discourse:** synopses and analyses of world affairs, politics, and social policy, which inform professional and civic life and often specific choices, such as voting. Public discourse includes news media; op-eds (opposite the editorial pages); general interest magazines (featuring long-form journalism); podcasts; social media; political debates; and community meetings and public hearings.
- **Forecasts and predictions:** economic forecasts and financial forecasts, which inform specific choices about investments, employment, purchases, and certain philanthropic decisions. Forecasts and predictions include macro-economic perspectives, individualized recommendations from financial planners, and recommendations from vendors, such as marketers, drawing on statistical analysis to project human behavior patterns.

- **Popular social science:** overarching theories of human behavior, which offer explanations of individual and group motivation, social-historical trends, such as polarization, and frameworks to ensure every decision is "right." Popular social science includes books on behavioral economics, social psychology, and organizational psychology, written by both researchers and journalists.

Simply identifying these categories can itself help you chart your course through the expert advice universe. You can think of these categories as a high-level map showing you the entities and objects you are meeting and need to navigate. However, as indicated earlier, the problem this book addresses is not simply people's sense of being overloaded by the volume of apparently credible expert points of view available today. The problem is more fundamentally that recommendations from credible sources tend to be superficial, overconfident, sometimes agenda-driven, and generally masking – rather than equipping you to navigate ambiguity and uncertainty. Consequently, categorizing expert perspectives does not provide you a detailed enough map for you to steer yourself successfully on your life's trajectory. To create the necessary, detailed map, I distilled my work with clients to create a conceptual toolkit, aligned with the categories of expert advice. The toolkit will aid you in getting what you need from credible sources, while enhancing your own capacity for reasoning and decision making. The toolkit employs concepts drawn the empiricist-analytic tradition of Western philosophy: theories of truth; a recognition of the limits of inductive reasoning; a pragmatic theory of knowledge; and an understanding of the techniques of ethical reasoning.

The tools are defined in more detail in the chapter summaries and key terms sections, below. I did not randomly choose these conceptual tools. Rather, I arrived at them empirically by testing them with my clients. To be candid, as with any empirical approach, I identified these intellectual practices through a process of trial and error with my clients. There were concepts and theories I suggested, which they did not find helpful. Through this iterative process, my clients concluded that the techniques outlined here brought them greater clarity, insight, and ultimately self-confidence and satisfaction with their actions and decisions. The concepts in the toolkit align with the categories of expert sources in this way:

- **Theories of truth** will help you decipher what is relevant for you in multiple modes of public discourse.
- **Recognizing the limits of induction** will help you accurately interpret forecasts and predictions.

- **A pragmatic theory of knowledge** will help you realistically interpret the findings and recommendations of popular social science.

While clients reported benefits both from categorizing sources of expert advice, and assessing those sources with the tools just described, they also experienced situations that could not be resolved by appeals to expert data and knowledge: personal dilemmas. For example, imagine you are in your late 30s. You have just married. You were also just diagnosed with a degenerative condition that could impede your parenting ability. Should you start a family? Expert medical advice can predict how your condition will advance, but it cannot indicate whether or not you should start a family. Only you and your partner's aspirations, self-awareness, and values can help you make this decision. Likewise, imagine you own a single-family rental property in a fairly affluent area, which is being re-zoned for higher density housing. Higher density zoning might allow for more affordable housing, but it also might negatively affect your property value. You wonder: should I support the change in zoning, or should I lobby against it? Like the previous dilemma, expert advice, for example statistics from various urban planners, might provide data for you to consider in your deliberations. Expert advice cannot, however, tell you what course of action will align with your own personal standards of, say, fairness. As in the previous situation, your determination of the right decision involves your own values, motivations, and aspirations.

These scenarios illustrate personal dilemmas, which by their very nature are beyond the purview of expert advice. Personal dilemmas necessarily require your personal judgment to make a decision that aligns with your hopes, goals, and values. To help my clients refine their personal judgment and resolve their personal dilemmas more satisfactorily, I introduced them to six types of ethical theory, which we adapted into a process of ethical reasoning. As with understanding theories of truth, recognizing the limitations of induction and the pragmatic theory of knowledge, clients reported that understanding ethical theories and applying ethical reasoning increased their confidence in their ability to resolve personal dilemmas and their satisfaction in the choices they made in response to their dilemmas.

How to Use This Book

This book functions as a handbook, meaning the chapters stand independently. You can read the book cover to cover, or you can select the topics that are of most interest to you. In other words, you can find the insights you need without necessarily reading the chapters in sequence.

The chapter are organized around the categories of expert advice just discussed. The conceptual tools are presented, as outlined above, as they are relevant to each particular category of expert advice. This introductory chapter concludes with a list of key terms and definitions, orienting you to the concepts in the rest of the book. It also concludes with a series of self-reflection questions, so that you can pinpoint what you hope to gain from your engagement with this book's content. The other chapters finish with tactical recommendations for practicing and applying the methods and techniques presented in each chapter. Likewise, each chapter concludes with a self-reflection journal designed to facilitate your growth by equipping you to track your progress, over a period of weeks, in implementing your new conceptual tools. Each journal also includes a self-efficacy scale, a tool to facilitate charting your increases in self-confidence. As you implement the practices shared in the chapters, you can self-assess the growth of your confidence in your ability to assess expert advice critically, navigate dilemmas, and make decisions. To sustain any change, we each need to track our progress. You may already do this for changes in habits, such as exercise and diet. Cognitive changes are no different. Routinely self-reflecting and self-assessing, using the guides in this book, will allow you to sustain changes in the way you reason, and facilitate improvements in your self-perception.

Although this book functions as a handbook, three themes run throughout the chapters. The first theme involves client stories. As indicated above, my interactions with clients have informed my understanding of the types of expert advice savvy professionals consult, and the reasons they consult it. Client stories thus form the backbone of this book. Each chapter includes narratives of clients either grappling with different forms of public discourse, seeking to understand forecasts, developing a realistic understanding of behavioral science claims, or navigating personal dilemmas. To be transparent, the clients described in the chapters, and my dialogue with them, do not represent specific individuals and verbatim conversations. Nonetheless, the clients described in this book are drawn from a number of real people and real conversations. I hope you can see yourself in these clients and that their experiences, concerns, questions, insights, and solutions resonate with you. Through the client stories, I will take you on a journey of sorts, showing you how we figured out the techniques, tools, and methods offered to you. In other words, the stories provide an immediate perspective into the ways this book's conceptual practices have been field-tested through real experiences.

The second theme, which will be apparent in the client stories, is tolerating and navigating, rather than denying uncertainty. As mentioned above, much expert advice sounds definitive. It provides assurances of certainty, promising to remove the discomfort of ambiguity and doubt with clear, simple solutions to complex situations. Yet, such solutions, rather than being elegant, are often merely simplistic, masking ambiguity and uncertainty. When, for instance, equally qualified experts come to very different conclusions, we see that uncertainty persists. In my experiences with clients, I have concluded that such oversimplification is a disservice. Regarding important life decisions, I have observed that thinking people receive the greatest benefit from information about alternatives and tools to determine their own actions, rather than directions regarding specifically what to choose and what to avoid in a given situation. Thinking people value their autonomy, and they often seek expert advice to experience greater autonomy by making better-informed choices. Perhaps ironically, expert advice can infringe on advice seekers' autonomy. Thus, rather than obscure uncertainty behind a mask of unconditional conclusiveness, this book provides techniques and methods to help you acknowledge and successfully navigate the uncertainty we all experience in various aspects of our lives.

Successfully navigating uncertainty relates to this book's third theme, refining your personal judgment. Perhaps the most rewarding aspect of my work with clients has been to support their development as astute thinkers and decision makers and to witness their reasoning abilities and self-confidence grow. Upon reflection, I realized that our work together ultimately resulted in their more refined personal judgment. Consequently, each of the conceptual practices offered in these chapters will help you enhance your personal judgment, increasing your capacity for independent thinking and self-direction. In turn, by employing these methods and tools, you can increase your self-confidence and satisfaction with your choices. To this end, the final chapter is distinct from the others. Because it examines dilemmas, rather than aligning a source of advice with relevant philosophical tools, the final chapter focuses more explicitly on methods to refine your personal judgment. Whilst you can read the final chapter on its own, it is designed to function as a capstone for this book.

To facilitate your using this book as a handbook, I offer the following chapter overviews. In Chapter 2, "What Does It Mean to Say Something Is True? Navigating Public Discourse," you will meet four clients, Carrie, Omar, Kim, and Delores. Carrie is a corporate executive and self-professed "infomaniac." Omar is a successful money manager who, when mid-career, pursued a civic leadership position. Kim, a serial entrepreneur, likewise pursued a community leadership position. Delores, a corporate executive, also served on a non-profit board. Each of their stories illustrates a different challenge navigating public discourse, ranging from news reports with fictional overtones, to conflicting expert opinions, to articles that mix findings from physical science with sociological interpretations. Through these stories, you will learn a method for navigating public discourse. The method begins with familiarizing yourself with modes of discourse generally and types of public discourse in particular. The method then involves understanding and employing a pluralistic view of truth. The chapter explains the difference between truth pluralism and relativism. The method continues with explaining the correspondence and coherence theories of truth. The correspondence theory is that something is true based on the degree to which it actually describes (corresponds to) something in the world. A correspondence theory may require that different people will make similar observations about a particular thing (say, a change in temperature), and that the similarity of their observations constitutes the truthfulness of the claim they make.

However, as truth pluralism demonstrates, not every claim or assertion can be true in the correspondence sense. Elements of public discourse that are interpretations – theories of history, social theories, ethics, aesthetics – often do not correspond directly to something real in world. In fact, pure mathematics cannot be demonstrated as true in the correspondence sense. While numbers, for instance can be applied to the real world through chemical or mechanical engineering formulas, numbers themselves are abstractions. Such abstractions and theories can nonetheless be true in the coherence sense, meaning the theories are internally coherent and align with other theories and interpretations of events. The stories of Carrie, Omar, Kim, and Delores illustrate how recognizing that different subjects are true in different ways can help you successfully navigate the ambiguities of public discourse.

In Chapter 3, "Is Forecasting Fortune Telling? The Limits of Moving from Specific to General," you will meet Lisa, an intellectually curious senior executive. She worked with a financial planner and wanted a clearer understanding of the planner's assertion, "You will be safe in retirement." Together, Lisa and I explored statistical forecasting methods. Similarly, you will meet Elliott, an executive with whom I partnered. Elliott sought a realistic understanding of a marketing vendor's claims to be able to nudge potential customers into making the decisions the vendor's clients wanted them to make.

Working as a thought partner to Lisa and Elliott, I realized that the expert perspectives we reviewed, which explained statistical modeling methods, left out a crucial point: all forecasts involve induction. Induction has a fundamental limitation. Induction is the process of drawing conclusions about a whole from a sample or part of a whole. Said differently, inductive reasoning is moving from specific cases, instances, or examples to general principles. It is a fundamental logical move of the scientific method.

Experiments produce samples of a certain phenomena. When these samples are replicated enough times, they suggest generalizations – for example, universal laws, such as the law of gravity. Consequently, induction is the essential logic of forecasting and predicting. The problem of induction is that speculating about *un*observed things based on things that we have observed does not give certainty about unobserved things; rather, it provides probabilities about the unobserved things. Understanding the statistical methods involved in forecasting and making predictions does not reveal this basic limitation of the methods themselves. Many people thus assume induction can produce certainty and purveyors of expert advice often reinforce this assumption (and they themselves may accept it). While this chapter makes you aware of the limitation of induction, it also provides tools to help you compensate for the limitation, such as practicing counterfactual and hypothetical thinking. These tools will help you get the most of forecasts, even while acknowledging they do not provide certainty.

In Chapter 4, "What Is an Idea's Cash Value? Behavioral Science and Pragmatism," you will meet Marc, a senior leader in a compliance department, who needed to help his staff be more creative and innovative. You will also meet Amanda, an entrepreneur who started her own aggregate recycling company. Amanda wanted to enhance her ability to pitch to clients, close deals, and retain clients for repeat business. Next, you will meet Mei, a leader who wanted to improve her interviewing and "people-reading" skills, to identify the best candidates for positions on her staff. Lastly, you will meet Juan, a senior HR leader, who wanted to change employees' behavior regarding their savings for retirement. Marc, Amanda, Mei, and Juan all consulted popular behavioral science sources for insights about influencing the behaviors of their employees, peers, and customers. Through my work with them, I developed tools specifically for assessing claims from behavioral science, a chief source of expert advice today.

In Chapter 4, you will learn how behavioral science – a cross-disciplinary field involving economics, cognitive psychology, social psychology, and sociology – has become a "hub science," and consequently a go-to source for advice seekers wanting insights regarding both macro- and micro-patterns of human behavior. The clients' stories illustrate that people consult behavioral sciences for professional reasons, for instance hoping there actually is a foolproof method of influencing consumer choices. They also consult behavioral science for personal, existential reasons, seeking a worldview to make sense of their experiences and reduce their anxieties.

Throughout the chapter, you will also become more aware of challenges involved with interpreting and implementing behavioral science findings. As with the forecasts and predictions examined in Chapter 3, people can be overconfident in the claims of behavioral science. They assume that, because it involves the scientific method of observation and experimentation, behavioral science provides infallible predictions of human behaviors and unerring techniques to influence other people's actions and choices. I have observed that this overconfidence may lead clients to oversimplify complex situations, and try to implement ineffective, if not counterproductive "interventions." Moreover, with my clients I have explored situations in which overconfidence in behavioral science may lead to a deterministic worldview, the perspective that all our actions are caused by factors beyond our control (for example, human evolution, genetics, or historical events). Embracing a deterministic worldview is problematic because it is disempowering. You may lose sight of your own and others' capacity for independent thought and action, which can result in self-doubt, ineffective decisions, or, worse, indecision.

As you read the client stories, you will also acquire the conceptual tools to manage the challenges that can emerge when assessing and employing ideas from behavioral science. The tools include recognizing the limitations of popular science books as a genre. Popular science authors frequently present scientific ideas as certainties, rather than as hypotheses, with often limited experimental evidence supporting them. Actual scientists are more circumspect about their findings. Similarly, popular science authors often emphasize extreme, unusual findings, which do not actually represent the consensus of scientists regarding a particular theory. A second tool involves understanding the foundational components of the scientific method, how these work in physical science, and where and when they may be misapplied in the social sciences. A third and crucial tool is recognizing the limits of induction, explored in Chapter 3. Behavioral science relies on induction: the move from a specific instance or example (established through an experiment or population survey) to a generalization about a population. The final tool is embracing the pragmatist theory of knowledge, which asserts that the value of conclusions and findings resides in their ability to solve practical, everyday problems. Assessing the claims of behavioral science using the pragmatic method allows you to identify how they can be best deployed, without being overconfident in them, assuming they represent transcendent, universal principles of human behaviors.

As mentioned above, Chapter 5, the final chapter, "How Do I Know I'm Doing the Right Thing? Trusting Your Own Judgment," does not examine a particular source of expert advice. Rather, it explores personal dilemmas, situations in which a choice ultimately involves your values, motivations, and life goals. People often associate the term dilemma with an explicitly ethical dilemma, which typically involves choosing between two ethically problematic courses of action. However, personal dilemmas are not always overtly ethical. They are characterized by tensions among goals, relationships, duties, and obligations. Because they involve our values and aspirations, dilemmas are in some sense beyond the purview of expert advice.

Chapter 5 presents an approach to refining your personal judgment by introducing you to four clients who experienced personal dilemmas. Simon, a biomedical researcher, faced a dilemma involving a career in public health and a career in private industry. Aviva, a non-profit executive director, faced a dilemma involving her fiduciary responsibility to the well-being of her organization and a crucial refugee resettlement initiative. Varsha, a corporate HR executive, faced a dilemma involving employee access to funding for MBAs. Matt, an engineer, attorney, and single parent, faced a dilemma involving his dream promotion to his firm's C-suite and parenting his adolescent children, while also caring for his father with dementia.

As I helped these clients deliberate, I realized they needed a framework to see how their values could inform their decisions. To create this framework, I introduced Simon, Aviva, Varsha, and Matt to six types of ethical theory. Using a reasoning method involving analogies, imagination, and empathy, they applied the six ethical theories to their dilemmas. They were able to resolve their dilemmas in ways that accorded with their own standards, and they experienced the satisfaction of having done the right thing to the best of their abilities. They also felt more confident in their ability to resolve future personal dilemmas.

Based on these stories, you will see that the approach to refining your personal judgment in Chapter 5 involves resolving dilemmas with a process of ethical reasoning. As mentioned above, with its specific focus on personal judgment, Chapter 5 serves as a capstone to the other chapters. It includes more in-depth self-awareness activities, such as a self-assessment of preferences for the six types of ethical theory presented in the chapter. It also includes dilemma case studies, which you can use to sharpen your ethical reasoning.

To conclude this introduction, I will paraphrase the way sociologist Robert Bellah and his colleagues ended their influential book, *Habits of the Heart*. In their appendix, "Social Science as Public Philosophy," they encouraged their readers to argue with them as authors, be candid about ideas and interpretations that did not fit well in the book's argument, and test the book's claims against their own lived experiences.[2] Given that my purpose is to help you enhance your capacity for independent thinking, and offer conceptual tools to support you being your own best guide and advocate, I invite you to do the same thing. As you embark on the journey this book represents, please argue with my assertions, candidly assess what tools and techniques are most relevant for you, identify those that are least useful, and test the practices and insights I developed with my clients against your own lived experiences. By engaging with the material in this way, you will begin to practice the essence of the methods this book recommends.

Orientation: Key Terms

Reviewing these terms will provide context for the conceptual tools presented in this book. The terms include both abstract ideas, such as "knowledge," specific subjects, such as "philosophy of science," and thought patterns, such as "inference." Familiarize yourself with these terms to orient yourself, charting the course you plan to take through this book.

Belief

As used in this book, the term belief combines psychological and philosophical definitions. Belief, for our purposes, is an attitude of being predisposed to accept a finding or claim as true, based on limited or preliminary evidence, anticipating that additional evidence will further validate the claim. As such, belief is a limited form of knowledge. This definition of belief contrasts with other definitions of belief as accepting something as true without evidence for it. As a type of knowledge, it is a foundation for applying the coherence theory of truth to public discourse, accepting forecasts as useful, rather than definitive predictions, and assessing findings presented by popular behavioral science using the pragmatic method.

Determinism

Determinism is a claim that all our choices and actions are inevitable responses to other causes and actions, and that our sense of making free choices is illusory. For our purposes, determinism cannot be empirically proven. Rather it is an inference drawn from or an interpretation of data, such as research about human genes or theories of evolution. As such, determinism is a metaphysical claim based on rational, abstract speculation.

Empiricism

Empiricism is the theory that knowledge is based on actual experiences, rather than abstract speculation. While the ancient Greek philosopher Aristotle is often cited as the first empiricist, the theory as known today developed in the sixteenth and seventeenth centuries. Along with induction, the theory is a foundation of the scientific method used in natural and social science. Empiricism involves observing events, such as weather, then developing theories to explain the events. It can also involve first creating a theory, then constructing an experiment to prove or disprove a theory. Many of the conceptual tools offered in the book come from empiricist philosophers, such as David Hume and William James.

Epistemology

Epistemology is the philosophical study of the ways we acquire knowledge, as well as what characteristics constitute knowledge. As a field of inquiry in Western thought, epistemology dates to ancient Greece. Likewise, epistemology is a field in philosophical traditions globally. In essence, this book is practical, applied epistemology. All the conceptual tools offered – theories of truth, recognizing the limits of induction, ethical theories – come from the discipline of epistemology, as it has developed in Western thought since the 1600s.

Induction

Induction is the process of inferring a generalization, for example a natural law, from specific instances and examples. Induction can be presented as the step from "observed As are Bs," to "therefore, all As whatsoever are Bs." Induction is the fundamental logical move of the scientific method, as used in natural sciences, social sciences, and statistics. Induction requires that, to develop knowledge, specific instances of "As are Bs" have to be observed numerous times, by different people in different locations, to justify the conclusion that all "As whatsoever are Bs." Induction thus depends on replication to create knowledge.

Inference

An inference is an assumption you make to draw connections between pieces of information for the purpose of coming to a conclusion. Inferences are not directly observable. Rather, we use them to make sense of what we directly observe. For example, drawing the conclusion "All dogs have fur," from the statements "All mammals have fur," and "All dogs are mammals" is a deductive inference. The statements "If it rains, the streets will be wet; it is raining, therefore the street is wet," represent a conditional inference.

Likewise, the inductive move from "some As are Bs" to "All As are Bs" involves an inference. Sometimes, inferences are mistaken, as illustrated by "If a fire hydrant is open, water will be running in the street; water is running in the street, therefore a fire hydrant is open." There are multiple reasons water could be running in the street. You cannot infer from seeing water in the street that a fire hydrant must be open. However, you could conjecture that a fire hydrant might be open.

Knowledge

Knowledge is often defined as your being aware of something based on your study or direct experience of that thing. This book defines knowledge not only as a mental state, but also as it relates to belief. Specifically, knowledge is belief that has been verified by a robust amount of evidence. In other words, knowledge is accepting as definitely true a claim that has been proven beyond a reasonable doubt. Knowledge is thus the strongest form of belief. You can obtain knowledge through both rational reflection and empirical observation. For example, mathematical knowledge results from rational reflection using deduction, while knowledge in the natural sciences typically results from empirical observation and induction.

Personal judgment

Personal judgment is a mutual-faceted thought process composed of several components. First, it involves your ability to distinguish your feelings from your thoughts, and to bracket emotional responses so that you are able to reason clearly. Second, it involves your ability to identify your intuitive or gut response to a situation, and likewise suspend the immediate judgment that intuitive responses represent. Intuitions and emotions are distinct. Intuitive or gut responses are actually rational responses, based on previous experiences. We experience intuition as automatic or reflexive, which makes it seem non-rational. Intuitive responses are, in fact, reasonable. However, they may not be relevant to your situation at hand. Third, personal judgment involves your ability to be aware of your own values, beliefs, goals, and aspirations. Finally, personal judgment is your ability to apply your self-awareness logically in specific situations to appraise information and evidence, drawing conclusions that inform your specific decisions and actions.

Philosophy of science

Philosophy of science is the source for several of the tools and techniques in this book. It dates back to the foundations of Western philosophy, when Plato and Aristotle first asked questions about the nature of scientific knowledge. Contemporary philosophy of science asks questions about assumptions underlying scientific methods. It also asks questions about the reliability of scientific theories, such as, "How do we know that experiments support the conclusions we draw from them?" Likewise, the philosophy of science explores how science shapes our understanding of our experiences, as well as how different cultural views have influenced the development of science. Philosophy of science does not deny science. Rather, its purpose is to clarify what we can know through science, and help us better detect pseudo-science.

Self-efficacy

Self-efficacy is your self-perception of your ability to master specific activities and tasks. We experience self-efficacy as feeling more or less competent to complete activities successfully in various aspects of our lives. Your sense of self-efficacy informs your perception of the power you have to achieve goals and aspirations, and thus to direct your own life.

Theory

A theory is a systematic explanation, often in the form of a framework, designed to bring coherence to various aspects of an experience, an event, or a body of knowledge, or to provide a solution to a fundamental problem. This book draws on various theories from philosophy, including theories of truth, and ethical theory. Theories of truth offer explanations describing the characteristics of truth, and how we can recognize what is truth in different situations. Ethical theories offer explanations regarding the origins of our conceptions of right and wrong, as well as what form action guides should take (for example, should they take the form of rules, or character development).

Uncertainty tolerance

People tolerate uncertainty differently in different aspects of their lives. A person who is self-employed may tolerate much uncertainty regarding their annual income (they may start each year not knowing how much they will earn), and may tolerate a little uncertainty regarding their vacations (they may need every hour of the trip planned).

As used in this book, uncertainty tolerance refers to your comfort in acknowledging that experts' assertions, findings, and conclusions, even when based on objective, empirical methods, may be evolving and subject to revision based on new evidence, rather than being definitive or absolute. Uncertainty tolerance enables you to evaluate sources of advice critically and judiciously, without falling into black-and-white interpretations, such as that a claim is totally true or totally false, totally right or totally wrong.

Reflection Questions

In addition to familiarizing yourself with the above terms, reflecting on these questions will help you chart your course through this book's content. The questions will also help you identify what thought processes and habits of mind you want to reinforce and change by engaging this book's concepts.

1. What attracted you to this book? What do you hope to gain by reading it (for instance, enhanced decision-making ability)?
2. What are your thinking and reasoning strengths? In what situations do you exercise them most effectively?
3. What aspects of your thinking and reasoning would you like to develop more? What situations pose challenges for your thinking and reasoning?
4. How satisfied do you feel with the most recent significant decision you made? In retrospect, what might you have done differently to achieve a more satisfying outcome?
5. How competent do you feel generally to pursue significant goals and aspirations? What leads you to this self-perception?
6. How empowered do you feel generally to pursue significant goals and aspirations? What leads you to this self-perception?
7. Chart your course for using this book. How do you plan to use it? Summarize in a few sentences what you hope to do differently after engaging this book's content.

Notes

1 For a fuller discussion about the enterprise of public philosophy, see Michael Sandel, *Public Philosophy: Essays on Morality in Politics* (Harvard University Press, 2008). For a description of experimental philosophy see J. Knobe, "Experimental Philosophy," *The Stanford Encyclopedia of Philosophy*, last updated December 19, 2017. https://plato.stanford.edu/entries/experimental-philosophy/.
2 Robert Bellah, Richard Madsen, William Sullivan, et al., *Habits of the Heart: Individualism and Commitment in American Life* (Harper and Row Publishers, 1986), 307.

Chapter 2

What Does It Mean to Say Something Is True?

Navigating Public Discourse

Chapter Outline

Introduction

When have you exclaimed, "I'm not sure what to think anymore"? Perhaps you said this to a conversation partner, or perhaps to yourself, under your breath. Consider the situations in which you have used this expression. What was the context? What were you experiencing? In my experience, people use such exclamations to express doubt, confusion, and sometimes frustration. In essence, such exclamations articulate a need for clarity. We often use such phrases in response to ambiguity that results from receiving conflicting pieces of information, or different, perhaps contradictory inter-pretations of the same information. For example, we might read in a finan-cial publication that a central bank is raising interest rates. One group of economists predicts that the increase will prevent inflation, while another group predicts the increase could slow growth to the point of a recession. Likewise, we might hear a radio news report describing two studies, both performed at respected university medical centers. One study finds that drinking wine has health benefits. The other study finds that drinking wine is associated with kidney disease. In the first example, experts with pre-sumably the same credentials make very different assessments of an event. In the second example, two different groups of experts, also presumably

DOI: 10.4324/9781003647034-2

with similar credentials, produce two very different pieces of data. In both cases, differing expert views create ambiguity, in response to which any of us might sigh and say, "I'm not sure what to think anymore."

I have observed though my work with individuals and groups in corporations, government agencies, and NGOs that people often encounter ambiguity in public discourse. While public discourse can include any exchange of ideas among friends, I find that people most often encounter ambiguity in forms of public discourse such as news media, social media, government public hearings, and some political speeches and debates. In all of these forms, you may encounter the ambiguity resulting from conflicting expert opinions, as illustrated in the above examples. However, conflicting expert views are not the only source of ambiguity. News media reports can mix fact-finding with storytelling in ways that cause ambiguity. The variety of communications that comprise public discourse itself – informative and explanatory, persuasive, or entertaining – can likewise create ambiguity. For some of us, ambiguity causes stress and anxiety, challenging a need we may have for predictability. It can thus impede our ability to be resilient. For others of us, ambiguity, because it interferes with our ability to make informed choices, can lead to postponing and, ultimately, avoiding decisions. Postponing and avoiding decisions leads to missed opportunities. Successfully navigating ambiguity is, therefore, crucial for actualizing the life you want to live, professionally and personally.

In this chapter, I will share a method of analysis I developed with clients, to help them navigate ambiguity, particularly as they have encountered it in public discourse. The method first involves techniques to identify the causes of ambiguity when you encounter it. The method next involves applying philosophical ideas about truth to sources of ambiguity. Specifically, I have encouraged clients to adopt a pluralistic view of truth: the findings and data of different domains can be true in different ways. (This is not a type of relativism or nihilism – pluralism does not claim that either everything is true or nothing is true.) From the pluralist perspective, for example, a law of physics is true in a way that differs from an historian's account of the causes of World War II. A medical diagnosis is true in way that differs from a political scientist's assessment of a particular candidate's success or failure in an election. Philosophers have developed additional theories of truth that can bring clarity to understanding specific types of public discourse. These include the correspondence and coherence theories of truth, both of which have been found by my clients to be useful tools for navigating the ambiguity that can occur in public discourse. Before sharing this method in more detail, however, I will first share client stories that illustrate different experiences of ambiguity in relation to public discourse. It is by working with these and similar clients that I developed the method I share in this chapter. Their stories also illustrate how to apply the method.

Clients Seeking Clarity

A participant in one of my critical thinking seminars, Carrie, contacted me afterward. An executive at a biomedical research organization, she wanted to work with me as her executive coach. Early in our work together, Carrie jokingly described herself as an "infomaniac news addict." Carrie held that keeping a close eye on current events was a key part of her success as an executive. It equipped her to anticipate trends and potential disruptions to her industry and organization.

In one of our monthly conversations, Carrie indicated she was troubled by a report she heard from a radio news source she had long trusted. She trusted the source because of its in-depth reporting and commitment to covering a topic for weeks, rather than days or hours. For instance, the source reported on the 2014 Ebola outbreak weeks before other major news outlets.

The report that troubled Carrie regarded a whistleblower who revealed a data breach at a federal agency. I asked Carrie to say more about what bothered her. As she elaborated, I realized that it was not just the content of the report – the data breach – that concerned her. She was also unsettled by the report's format.

Carrie explained that the report started with a story about a day in the life of the whistleblower, culminating in the whistleblower's resolution to contact a journalist about the data breach. Carrie explained further that the report had a conspiratorial tone, and ended with the ominous question, "Who knows how many citizens' personal data – including social security numbers – are now at risk?"

Carrie observed, "I think of the news as a witness to events. Like a witness in a trial when I've been on a jury, I count on my news sources to provide me basic facts." She concluded, "What am I supposed to do with that last question – 'Who knows how many citizens are at risk?' That's not factual, it doesn't tell me anything." Carrie chuckled, "I can hear Perry Mason objecting to that report as speculation on the part of the witness." Carrie then expressed frustration, "The news from this radio station has always been so dependable. This report seemed to be about emotions and moods, not facts and events."

I had a similar conversation with another client, Omar, a successful money manager. We met through a referral from another of my clients. At mid-career, Omar wanted to become more involved in his community. He had volunteered for several non-profit organizations, and decided to pursue a more strategic role, with the potential to create systemic change. To this end, he accepted an appointment to the board of his region's transportation authority. The board was empowered to approve new initiatives the authority could implement. Omar felt the board membership was the perfect fit for him.

Part of the authority's strategic plan, approved before Omar joined the board, was to reduce the number of individual drivers commuting to work on local freeways. The authority asked the board to consider several initiatives, including the creation of express bus lines. The express bus plan involved building satellite parking lots in suburban areas, and establishing express bus lanes on main thoroughfares that connected the suburban areas to the urban core. The goal was to make bus service more efficient for commuters, and thus induce more commuters to use mass transit. The project would cost approximately $53 million dollars.

I met with Omar not long after he heard presentations and read reports compiled by two nationally recognized public transportation experts, both of whom had helped other regions successfully reduce freeway traffic by implementing express bus services. When I inquired about the meeting, Omar explained that one expert provided data showing the express bus service would reduce the number of individual drivers using local expressways by 20 percent. But, he continued, "the other expert said that the express bus service would have little to no impact on people's preference for mass transit." Omar added, "The second expert basically said the express buses would do more harm than good because they would displace routes needed by current bus riders, who typically don't own cars. With express buses, we would end up with less bus usage than there is now." Omar indicated he was puzzled that two experts with similar credentials, in the same field, came to such different conclusions. "It seems like," he observed, "people using the same methods would come to more or less the same conclusions. I thought we would be using their data to tweak our idea. Now it seems like the second expert is calling into question the whole concept." Omar further expressed frustration, saying, "In finance, everything seems so much more black-and-white. I now just feel confused – maybe I'm not the right person for this board." Where Carrie experienced ambiguity due to the way a single, trusted source brokered information she expected to be factual, Omar experienced ambiguity when two similar expert sources came to very different conclusions, presumably using similar methods and data.

Another client, Kim, had an experience similar to Omar's. Kim was a serial entrepreneur who approached me after a seeing me give a keynote talk. Like Omar she wanted to engage me as a thought partner. Also like Omar Kim pursued community leadership roles, the first of which was serving on the board of her neighborhood association. Kim's neighborhood was adjacent to wetlands and its streets were prone to flooding, although the flooding did not seem to follow a consistent pattern. To address the problem, the board sought a proposal from an environmental engineer, who had developed a rain gauge that very effectively predicted the likelihood of the flooding of specific areas whenever rain fell. The gauge could be connected to other equipment that would produce early warnings if flooding was likely.

In one of our conversations, Kim explained that the board also decided to commission a report from a biologist specializing in wetland habitats. The biologist's report indicated that the installation of the rain gauges would interfere with the nesting habits of certain waterfowl that used the wetlands for breeding and raising their young. Kim explained, "We are in a real quandary, you know? We need to get a handle on this flooding because it's starting to affect our property values, and nobody wants to spend the money to regrade all the streets." She said further, "But, one reason people like our neighborhood, and one reason our homes have appreciated quite a bit, is the ability to view the wildlife in the wetlands. So, we don't want to hurt any of the animals or discourage them from living near us." I asked if the board had investigated other ways to manage the flooding hazard. She explained, "Basically, the two options are either change the roads, or predict which roads are flooding, so people can use different roads. Identifying which roads are flooding so people can plan accordingly is much less expensive. I think that's the way the board has to go." Kim's situation reminded me of Omar. Kim experienced ambiguity when faced with two apparently conflicting expert opinions. In Kim's case, however, the experts were from different disciplines and they were focused on different concerns: the engineer was focused on generating accurate flood warnings, while the biologist was focused on the impact of a specific technology on wildlife habitat.

A fourth client, Delores, became a long-term coaching client after meeting me at a critical thinking seminar I facilitated. Delores was an executive in a manufacturing company, and a board member of a human services non-profit. She was similar to Kim and Omar in wanting to serve her community in a strategic way. Committed to being well informed in both her professional and civic work, she read widely about social and political issues. In one of our conversations, she shared that she had encountered a concept that was new for her. In an article in a popular monthly science magazine, Delores read that a number of biologists were recommending that racial categories be phased out of genetic research.[1] Delores explained further that, according to the biologists, race is a concept that can have social meaning, but that it interferes with a scientific understanding of genetics. After reading this article, Delores continued, she searched for more articles about the idea that race has social, rather than biological meaning. Her search led her to a number of articles in newspapers she respected. Some of the newspaper articles were op-eds while others were in the science sections of publications. Delores observed, "I want to understand these concepts, but I'm not sure how these ideas relate. How does the genetic research I started with relate to the theories I am reading about that are social constructs?" I heard in Delores's question an articulation of ambiguity. In some ways, the source of Delores' sense of ambiguity was similar to Kim's. Kim encountered experts from two different disciplines providing data on two different aspects of the same situation. Similarly, Delores encountered claims based on ideas from two different domains, natural science (specifically genetics) and social science (specifically sociology). That Delores experienced ambiguity may be surprising, given that concepts from both domains were used to support the same conclusion. Even though both domains share certain empirical methods, such as observation and experiments, and both seek to identify causal explanations that are generalizable, they apply them to very different things. Genes are more precisely observable and quantifiable than individual and collective human behavior. Consequently, Delores experienced the ambiguity that can result from applying assumptions and frameworks from one field to another.

Dissecting Public Discourse

The four clients I just described were savvy consumers of information when we started working together. For instance, they could identify sources that tended to be echo chambers, such as certain social media platforms.[2] They engaged with these sources for entertainment, but did not consult them expecting objective information to inform actions and decisions. Carrie, Omar, Kim, and Delores were also aware that some sources, such as political debates, are intended to persuade their audiences. These clients certainly watched political debates, but they expected that each candidate's goal was to persuade voters to vote for them. Thus, these clients anticipated that candidates might oversimplify and exaggerate, and they were prepared to fact-check what candidates said.

I noticed that my clients typically did not experience ambiguity when engaging a form of public discourse that they perceived as intended to be persuasive or to reinforce views they already held, such as social media sources. In other words, public discourse, per se, did not stimulate ambiguity. However, clients did experience ambiguity when they consulted a source that they expected to provide objective information and they received something different: either the information seemed non-objective (designed to illicit emotion, for instance) or the information was objective, yet seemed to contradict itself or to support different, often opposed courses of action.

As I worked with Carrie, Omar, Kim, Delores, and other clients, I developed an analytical method to address the ambiguity that can occur when a source consulted for objective information does not provide clarity. The first part of the method is to be aware of the modes of discourse and forms of public discourse. While discourse can be any kind of written or spoken communication, it generally falls into four categories: description, exposition, argumentation, and narration.[3] *Description*'s purpose is to make you aware of the sensory aspects of a situation. For example, a reporter covering a natural disaster or a political convention will vividly describe sounds, smells, and sights to give you a sense of people's lived experiences "on the ground."[4] Such descriptions can help you imagine yourself in the actual situation. *Exposition*'s purpose is to convey information by defining terms, brokering facts, analyzing and summarizing reports, sources, or events.[5] For example, a reporter discussing a United States Supreme Court decision will explain how different justices voted, and summarize both the majority and dissenting opinions. *Argumentation*'s purpose is to change your mind, your point of view, your attitude, and/or your feelings about a person, issue or event.[6] For example, the author of a newspaper op-ed will organize information in such a way as to support a particular interpretation of the information, and may use the interpretation as evidence justifying a call to action. *Narration*'s purpose is to give you an impression of an event, a moment in time, conveying to you what happened and how it happened.[7] For instance, the author of a long-form journalism article, say about civil unrest in a developing country, may organize the article around the perceptions of a particular real person, developing that person into a character.

In addition to recognizing the four modes of discourse, I have learned with my clients that identifying forms of specifically public discourse is similarly useful. Forms of public discourse include informing, persuading, and entertaining.[8] Carrie, Omar, Kim, and Delores already had some understanding of these forms, as demonstrated by their selective engagement with social media and caution regarding sources such as political debates. These forms overlap with the traditional four modes of discourse. *Informing* involves the modes of exposition and description; *persuading* involves the modes of argumentation and description; and *entertaining* involves the modes of narrative and description. Recognizing these forms of public discourse, and how they relate to the modes of discourse, has helped my clients effectively navigate ambiguity by helping them dissect specific sources, particularly those sources they expect to provide objective, clarifying information.

As illustrated by the client experiences I have shared, ambiguity frequently occurs because a source mixes the modes of discourse. For instance, a source we assume is intended to inform, and that we expect to use exposition and description, may also use narration, making it hard to identify the facts we seek. Carrie's experience of the radio news report regarding the data breach illustrates this. Carrie expected this source to provide, as she said, a form of eyewitness testimony. In other words, she consulted the source for information, which she expected to be delivered by means of exposition, with enough description to contextualize the exposition. Carrie was confused when the source included vivid personal descriptions and narrative, presenting the whistleblower as a character in a story, and ending the report with a suspenseful question. The mixed modes of discourse created ambiguity for Carrie, and she did not perceive the objective information she was seeking.[9] As I learned when working with Carrie and similar clients, awareness of the modes of discourse can provide clarity in these more subtle situations. By understanding the distinctions, particularly between exposition, description, and narration, you can determine why a particular source strikes you as ambiguous. For example, you can look and listen for clues, such as the development of characters and emotionally stimulating descriptions. Such clues indicate that a source, which you expect to provide objective information mainly through exposition, has mixed narrative into its reports, likely for the purpose of entertainment. Recognizing such clues, you can address ambiguity by filtering out the narrative and too-vivid descriptions, zeroing in on the objective information embedded in the narrative.

While awareness of the four modes of discourse and the modes of public discourse allows you to correct for ambiguity caused by mixing modes of discourse, it does not address the ambiguity resulting from conflicting expert perspectives, illustrated by the stories of Omar, Kim, and Delores. Thus, the analytical method I developed with my clients includes a second component: applying theories of truth to aspects of public discourse.

Theories of Truth

If you are like my clients, the phrase "theories of truth" may sound self-contradictory. I remember Carrie's response to this phrase. She exclaimed, "How can truth be a theory? Truth just *is*. It's a black or white thing. Something is either true or false." Omar, Kim, and Delores had similar responses. Carrie's comment expresses the concern that saying there are different theories of truth sounds like saying either "everything is true" or "nothing is true." While there are philosophical positions that assert both of these, relativism (everything can be true, truth is subjective) and nihilism (truth does not exist), examining the truth from a theoretical perspective does not involve taking either position. From a philosophical perspective, theories of truth answer important questions: What qualities make something true? And how do we know something is true? Reflecting on philosophical answers to these questions has helped my clients negotiate the ambiguity that can arise from apparently conflicting expert sources.

The first theory of truth I recommended to Carrie, Omar, Kim, Delores, and other clients answers the question: What makes something true? The theory is often called truth pluralism. Truth pluralism's answer to this question is that the characteristics of truth vary by domain, field, or subject. In other words, from the perspective of truth pluralism, different subjects (for example, natural sciences, social sciences, mathematics, and law) each recognize different qualities as making something true.[10] The way a postulate is true in math is different from the way a law is true in physics, a theorem is true in economics, and principles are true in legal reasoning. Some philosophers claim that every domain has its own characteristics of truth, while other philosophers claim that all domains share certain characteristics of truth.[11] To use truth pluralism as a tool for maneuvering around the ambiguities of public discourse, we do not need to pick a side in this debate. The key is to embrace the idea that characteristics of truth can vary across domains. Embracing this, however, may require some preliminary cognitive work. When introducing clients to this approach, I learned that accepting truth pluralism often involves a shift in perspective, if not mindset. This is because most of us hold that there is a single, universal standard of truth (many philosophers hold this as well, although they disagree about what this standard is).[12] For example, Omar's initial response to truth pluralism was, "It just sounds like a version of relativism. How is saying different domains have different ways of establishing truth any different from saying truth is subjective and anything can be true if you want it to be." In response, I emphasized that truth pluralism, in contrast to relativism, does not deny the existence of objective truth; rather, it holds that truth has different attributes in different areas of our experience.

To shift their perspectives regarding what constitutes truth, I have asked clients to consider analogies that illustrate how characteristics of truth can vary across domains. I invite you to consider them, as well. First, imagine a trip you make to the grocery store from your house. There are probably several routes you can take, although one particular route may be better than another based on specific criteria. For instance, one route may be the fastest. Another route may be the most scenic. A third route might take you past other places you need to visit, such as the post office or dry cleaners. Although these routes differ in characteristics, they are all true in that they will get you to the grocery store. There are also clearly "false" routes that will not take you to the grocery store. Consider another, slightly more technical analogy: engineers designing a bridge, a car, or a phone. There are multiple effective designs for each of these. Some designs may meet certain client criteria, such as costs or timelines, better than others. Nonetheless, a variety of engineering solutions can be true when addressing a specific problem or creating an innovation.[13] There are also plenty of ideas that will be "false," in that they do not solve a particular problem. I have invited my clients to create their own analogies, and I invite you to do the same. Imagine situations in your life in which there are multiple valid solutions to a specific problem. Truth pluralism works the same way. When you are able to imagine situations in which you already recognize that multiple things can equally well solve a problem, such as routes to a store, you can understand how pluralism functions. Truth pluralism takes a perception you already employ routinely and applies it more broadly. As the analogies illustrate, truth pluralism still allows you to identify what is false.

After Omar, Kim, Carrie, Delores, and other clients shifted their perception of what makes truth "truth," they recognized the usefulness of truth pluralism in navigating ambiguity in public discourse. For example, recognizing that specific properties make something true in a particular domain helped them avoid misconceptions that may arise when applying the characteristics of truth from one domain, say natural sciences, to another domain seeking to understand very different subject matter, say sociology. While useful, truth pluralism by itself does not explain *how* things are true *in specific domains*. Truth pluralism provides a framework. In other words, pluralism might be called a meta-theory of truth. By itself, however, truth pluralism won't help you navigate some of the specific causes of ambiguity my clients experienced, such as that caused by conflicting expert findings. Thus, I introduced my clients to additional philosophical theories of truth: the correspondence theory and the coherence theory. Where truth pluralism asserts that domains have different characteristics of truth, correspondence and coherence theories go into more detail about specific characteristics of truth. Philosophers typically advocate that either correspondence or coherence is the most accurate account of what constitutes truth, although some truth pluralists suggest that both theories can be accurate ways to describe the attributes of truth in different domains. Building on the foundation of truth pluralism, for our purposes, both correspondence and coherence theories are helpful in practical terms for reducing the ambiguity you may experience when assessing specific sources in public discourse.

Most people I have met in seminars, presentations, and when coaching clients would say correspondence is *the* accurate description of truth. The correspondence theory is that something is true based on the degree to which it actually describes (corresponds to) something in reality. Many philosophers credit the twentieth-century British philosopher Bertrand Russell with the first full articulation of the correspondence theory. Russell asserted that beliefs are true when there are corresponding facts, and they are false when there are no corresponding facts.[14] Russell's theory can be represented as: x is true if and only if x corresponds to some fact; x is false if and only if x does not correspond to any fact. According to the correspondence theory, a "fact" is a real state of affairs, the thing in the world (event, statement, physical law, etc.), that exists independently of our thoughts or language. A statement is true if it accurately describes that real state of affairs or thing in the world. In contrast, a false statement does not accurately reflect a real state of affairs. Falsehood either misrepresents a real state of affairs or describes a state of affairs that does not exist.

Some aspects of our experience are clearly true in the correspondence sense.[15] Assertions about the physical world, for instance, are true in the correspondence sense. To say, "The package is somewhere between Phoenix and Las Vegas," corresponds to the physical location of the package. To say "I left her a message yesterday morning and she did not return my call," corresponds to a physical transaction among electronic circuits, that provide evidence of a message transmitted and saved. Likewise, medical information is true in the correspondence sense. An MRI (magnetic resonance imaging) scan shows the physical location of lesions on an individual's brain. A blood test can show the physical presence of certain types of fats in an individual's blood.

Applied to sources of public discourse, the correspondence theory of truth is relevant, for example, to conclusions from the natural sciences. A genome is a physical object, although microscopic, which exists in the nucleus of a cell. When a researcher or policy analyst refers to genomes, they are speaking about specific physical objects, with specific physical locations, which have been observed by many researchers for many years. Similarly, the assertions of quantum mechanics can be true in the correspondence sense – the assertions describe subatomic physical activity, which many different people have observed, for a number of years. The extinction of a specific species can be described as true by the correspondence theory. Taxidermy dodo birds are evidence that dodos once existed; and there are numerous human records documenting the existence of dodos.

The examples I have just cited probably seem straightforward, not ambiguous. However, ambiguity can emerge in the previous examples: for instance, if radiologists disagree about what they see in a particular MRI, or physicists disagree about the correct interpretation of the results of an experiment. In other words, when experts differ in their interpretation of evidence that is true by the correspondence sense, ambiguity may result. To understand how the correspondence theory can help navigate such ambiguity in public discourse, let us return to the stories of my clients Omar and Kim. Omar experienced ambiguity when experts from the same domains, urban transportation planning, came to different conclusions regarding the same proposed plan, an express bus service. One expert provided data showing an express bus service would reduce the number of individual drivers using local expressways by 20 percent, while the other expert said that the express bus service would not significantly reduce the number of individual drivers on local freeways.

Kim experienced ambiguity when experts from two different domains, an environmental engineer and a biologist, provided data that seemed to conflict. Deploying rain gauges recommended by the engineer, would, according to the biologist, disrupt the breeding patterns of local wildlife. To address the ambiguity each encountered, I first suggested that Omar and Kim ask themselves in what way the claims of each expert could be true. Kim concluded that the claims of both experts, although they were from different domains, could be true in the correspondence sense. The claims about the effectiveness of the rain gauge should correspond to facts and the claims of the biologist should correspond to facts. From this conclusion, Kim saw that she could address the ambiguity of the conflicting expert opinions by determining, through additional research, which expert's statements most closely corresponded to the facts – the real state of affairs – each was describing.

Omar concluded that some of the claims of each expert could be true in the correspondence sense. Each expert's data about actual localities implementing an express bus service should correspond to facts – the real state of affairs – in each locality. Omar also recognized that there was an aspect of each expert's claims that could not be true in the correspondence sense because the claims were based on projections into the future. Because, by definition, the future has not yet occurred, projections and predictions cannot be true in the correspondence sense (there is not yet a reality for them to correspond or fail to correspond to). Nonetheless, the data on which the projections are based can be true in the correspondence sense. In Omar's case, identifying what in the experts' claims could be true by correspondence, and what could not, helped him identify different questions to ask each expert. It also helped him identify additional methods he could use to assess their claims (the next chapter addresses these additional methods for assessing projections and predictions).[16] In Kim's case, identifying that both expert's claims could be true by correspondence helped her identify her next step, further research. It also helped her realize that she was not faced with competing expert claims; rather she was faced with different courses of action (deploy rain gauges or protect wildlife), each with its own costs and benefits. This realization, in turn, enabled her to reframe the discussion with her neighborhood association. Rather than be confused by apparently conflicting experts, Kim's association was able to focus on decision making and seeking a solution that might achieve both goals of more accurate flood prediction and wildlife protection.

The stories of Omar and Kim illustrate that applying the correspondence theory to certain forms of public discourse addresses ambiguity by offering a standard for determining which expert claims are closer to the truth based on evidence. By providing you with a scale of sorts – which claim seems closest to the truth – the correspondence theory also allows you to recognize that a conclusion or theory can be mainly true; it does not have to be true in every case to be useful in helping to solve a problem. (If you have been involved in legal procedures, you may be familiar with a similar concept of degrees of truth: proof beyond a reasonable doubt, proof based on a preponderance of the evidence, proof based on clear and convincing evidence, and so forth.) Moreover, recognizing what cannot be true by correspondence creates the opportunity to reframe a problem and identify different approaches to resolving the problem. Similar to Omar and Kim, Carrie also found the correspondence theory useful in her analysis of news media. Once she filtered out narrative material intended to persuade or entertain, she used the correspondence theory to assess the veracity of events reported by various news outlets. In her words, the correspondence theory helped her better assess the quality of the "eyewitness testimony" she expected from her trusted news sources.

However, as suggested by truth pluralism, not every claim or assertion can be true in the sense of correspondence. To illustrate this, let's return to Delores' story. When reading an article about genetics, written about four geneticists who asserted race was not a useful scientific category, Delores experienced ambiguity. As described in the article, the researchers linked claims from their biological research to a sociological theory often called social constructionism.[17] When she first read this article, Delores experienced ambiguity because the article drew on multiple domains, and she (like Carrie, Kim, and Omar) assumed that all domains share the same truth characteristics. As just discussed, embracing truth pluralism addresses this type of ambiguity to an extent. When Delores applied truth pluralism to the article, she was able to tackle the ambiguity she experienced, first by asking can genetics and social constructionism be true in the same way. Her answer was, *maybe*. To clarify further, Delores then applied the correspondence theory of truth to her source. She concluded that her source's claims about the similarities and differences in genes among geographically disparate people could be proved or disproved by physical, albeit microscopic, evidence. In other words, the genetic claims could be true in the correspondence sense. However, Delores did not think the sociological claims could be true in the correspondence sense. She remarked, "I'm not sure how the claim that *x* or *y* is a construct can be verified in the same way as a biological hypothesis."

Delores put her finger on a limitation of the correspondence theory of truth as a tool for navigating ambiguity in public discourse. There are a number of domains in which claims cannot be demonstrated as true in the correspondence sense. (This is the reason that embracing truth pluralism is the *beginning* of the method for navigating ambiguous parts of public discourse, which I developed with my clients.) Thus, I shared a third theory, the coherence theory of truth, with Delores and others. Philosophers developed the coherence theory of truth to explain how certain statements and ideas, such as "a triangle has three sides" and "2 + 2 = 4" are true.[18] In philosophy, the examples I just cited are called *a priori* or analytic statements, meaning statements based purely on logical deduction. In other words, such abstract statements are true, not through observation or experimentation, but by definition or through logical reasoning. Since analytical claims are not observable in the way, say, the law of gravity is observable, it is difficult to say that analytic statements are true in the correspondence sense (although their truth can be demonstrated through their application in particular fields, such as engineering).

To explain how analytic statements are true, philosophers articulating the coherence theory of truth assert that assessing a claim or statement as true or false is saying that it coheres, or does not cohere, with a system of other logically implied statements. Thus, for example, 2 + 2 = 4 is true in the coherence sense, because its elements are interdependent with the meaning and truth of all the other statements of the arithmetical system. While certain claims, such as "Mount Everest is over 29,000 feet tall," are true because they correspond to something actual in the world, other abstract claims, such as "there is a color blue, and another color red" are true because they cohere (and do not contradict each other) as elements in a system. By proposing that analytic statements cannot be true in the same way as empirical observations, the coherence theory of truth supports the view that truth has different attributes in different domains.

To see more practically how you can apply the coherence theory of truth in everyday matters, suppose you are a small business owner and you engage a marketing company. The marketing company gives you a logo, asserting it is perfect for you. The marketers received positive feedback on the logo from all your current customers, and from a number of leads you hope to convert to customers. "This logo is perfect for you," is a truth statement, in that it coherently summarizes the data collected about the logo. However, the claim "this logo is perfect for you" is also implicitly a prediction. Thus, you cannot know it is true in the correspondence sense until you see the sales results it produces.

In trying to understand the coherence theory, Delores observed, "It seems like a lot of statements I would call interpretations can't be true in the correspondence sense, but they can be true in the coherence sense." Delores' observation was on target. Often in public discourse, even in sources we turn to for objective information, we encounter not just facts, but interpretations of facts. It can be a challenge to demonstrate that interpretations are true in the correspondence sense, although you can assess their truth in the coherence sense.

Delores and I discussed, for instance, that it is difficult to demonstrate how certain historical theories are true in the correspondence sense. Like Delores, you might encounter theories of history when seeking insights to enhance your practice of leadership. The occurrence of a battle can be demonstrated in the correspondence sense with archeological evidence. The existence of historical figures can be demonstrated in the correspondence sense, for example if their remains can be identified and their written works survive. In contrast, a historical leadership theory, such as the "great person theory of history" is difficult to prove in the correspondence sense.[19] This theory asserts that the course of history has been primarily influenced by individual leaders, innovators, and heroes, rather than political or cultural movements. Although the existence of specific leaders from different epochs can be true in the correspondence sense, the claim that history is shaped by the actions and decisions of certain extraordinary persons cannot be proved in the correspondence sense. The events that one historian would use to demonstrate the great person theory could be used by another historian to support a completely different theory (such as a Marxist analysis of history, which suggests changes occur mainly due to class conflicts).

I shared with Delores the work of a particular coherence theorist, the British twentieth-century philosopher F. H. Bradley. Bradley's thoughts helped Delores understand how to use the coherence theory to appraise interpretations in public discourse. Interpretations and theories may not be empirically verifiable in the correspondence sense (as is the claim Mt. Everest is over 29,000 feet tall), nor are they analytic (as is the claim a triangle has three sides). Bradley used the coherence theory particularly to assess the veracity of interpretations of historical events. He asserted that theories of history are historians' rational constructions, similar to analytic truths, rather than being based on direct observation of events.[20] For Bradley, a claim about history is true if it coheres with a broader system of interpretations of the past. To practice using this technique, Delores asked of the great person theory, "How does this theory cohere with the other theories about change over the course of history?" Delores concluded that the great person theory could not be absolutely true in the coherence sense, because there are other competing theories that use the same evidence to arrive at different conclusions. Delores observed the great person theory could be partly true – change sometimes could be due to certain individual leaders.

I asked Delores how she thought the coherence theory of truth could help her address the ambiguity she experienced when she read the article drawing on both genetics (biology) and social construct theory (sociology). As noted earlier, Delores recognized that the correspondence theory of truth could help her assess the article's biological claims about genetic differences among groups of people. She further observed, "I can use the coherence theory of truth to assess the sociological claims. I see them as interpretations, similar to the theories of history we have been talking about." Delores added, "I can first assess the sociological theories in terms of their own internal consistency. I can analyze how well the theories hang together and whether they contradict themselves at any point." She stated further, "I can also consider how the specific claims in the article fit with other social theories, looking for how they align or do not align with other theories."

A few conversations later, Delores circled back to our discussions about the correspondence and coherence theories of truth. She had noticed that the correspondence theory created for her a false dichotomy. According to the correspondence theory, if a claim does not correspond directly to some aspect of reality, it is automatically false. Yet, as illustrated by abstractions such as numbers and colors, some things are true, even if they cannot be demonstrated as such by correspondence. Dolores explained that, due to its potential true/false dichotomy, correspondence theory did not give her any perspective on a particular framework, social construct theory, she wanted to understand better. In contrast, the coherence theory provided criteria for her to appraise the framework. Dolores reflected further, "Learning about the coherence theory was really helpful, because a lot of public discourse involves not just brokering facts, but someone's interpretation of the facts' significance, such as what they might mean in the future."

Carrie, Omar, and Kim echoed Delores' thoughts. While Carrie employed the correspondence theory of truth to assess the facticity of news media reports, she found applying the coherence theory to narrative forms present in public discourse helped her gain insights she might otherwise have missed about possible repercussions of events. Omar and Kim also encountered situations in which they had to parse interpretive theories. In these situations, they found the coherence theory of truth proved to be more relevant than the correspondence theory. All four clients, as well as others, reported that embracing truth pluralism, as well as the correspondence and coherence theories of truth, enabled them to distill more effectively the insights and guidance they were seeking from public discourse.

Toolkit for Navigating Public Discourse

Tool 1: The Five-Step Method for Addressing Ambiguities in Public Discourse

1. Determine which mode of discourse a particular source represents: description, exposition, narration, or argumentation.
2. Determine which category of public discourse a particular source belongs to: informing, persuading, entertaining.
3. Consider that a particular source may mix modes of discourse, for example exposition and entertainment. Be clear about what you want to gain from the source and filter out material, such as narrative, that may not be relevant for your purpose.
4. Embrace truth pluralism: recognize that different domains, such as natural sciences, social sciences, mathematics, law, and art have different criteria for establishing truth.
5. Apply the correspondence and coherence theories of truth to the information a source provides. Bear in mind what types of information can generally be assessed by correspondence, for example a biological process, and what types of information can generally be assessed by coherence, for example interpretive theories.

Tool 2: Develop the Mindset for Truth Pluralism

As mentioned, to embrace truth pluralism, clients sometimes needed to shift their perspective, if they had assumed truth is defined by a single set of criteria across disciplines. To develop a mindset for truth pluralism, try the following techniques:

- Identify where you already employ the idea that several things can be true at the same time. We express truth pluralism every day when we use expressions such as "There is more than one way to cook an egg," and "All roads lead to Rome." Look for occasions in your routine activities in which you can see multiple, equally effective solutions to a single problem.

- Practice your ability to reason by analogy. For example, take the plot of a story you enjoy and reset it in a new, different setting. How might you reset a Sherlock Holmes mystery in a modern research hospital? How might you reset *Romeo and Juliette* on a space station? Such activities help you abstract essential elements from specific circumstances. Enhancing your ability to abstract can, in turn, help you become comfortable with the idea that different domains have different standards for truth (although they all have standards).

Tool 3: Deliberately Engage Unfamiliar Subjects

To enhance both your ability to apply the five-step method outlined above and develop your mindset for truth pluralism, seek out subjects and fields you do not typically go to for information. While you do not need to abandon your trusted sources of public discourse, you can build conceptual agility by continually researching new sources, intentionally challenging ideas you have come to accept. Seeking new sources of information involves intentionally putting yourself in the (sometimes uncomfortable) position of navigating what is unknown to you. For instance, if you have a background in science or engineering, try reading or listening to sources in art history and social theory. If you have a background in literature, try reading or listening to sources in social science disciplines, such as psychology or economic theory. The process of sifting through new information to discern what you find credible, relevant, useful, and useless keeps you poised to adapt to new situations, both professional and personal, that inevitably are part of everyone's experience. Exposing yourself to topics and fields you do not know well creates occasions to practice applying theories of truth.

Progress Journal

You can sustain changes in your thinking in a similar way to the way you might change habits, such as what you eat and how much you exercise. Track your progress by keeping a journal of how you implement new ideas, noting which are easy to apply and where you run into challenges.

Progress Journal – Week 1

Weekly Self-Reflection

- What modes and categories of public discourse did you encounter this week (such as exposition, narration, persuasion)?
- Which tools did you apply to analyze a source in public discourse (such as applying the coherence theory of truth)?
- What insights did you gain about the situation the source was addressing?
- What difference did this insight make to a problem you needed to solve or a decision you needed to make?

Pulse-Check

0	1	2	3	4	5	6	7	8	9	10
Not at all					Somewhat					Absolutely

Using the scale given above, rate your degree of confidence below by recording a number from 0 to 10 in the column on the right.

Please rate how confident you are that you can:

Identify a source's mode of discourse	
Identify the type of public discourse to which a source belongs	
Manage any discomfort associated with applying truth pluralism	
Appraise a source using the correspondence theory of truth	
Appraise a source using the coherence theory of truth	

Progress Journal – Week 2

Weekly Self-Reflection

- What modes and categories of public discourse did you encounter this week (such as exposition, narration, persuasion)?
- Which tools did you apply to analyze a source in public discourse (such as applying the coherence theory of truth)?
- What insights did you gain about the situation the source was addressing?
- What difference did this insight make to a problem you needed to solve or a decision you needed to make?

Pulse-Check

0	1	2	3	4	5	6	7	8	9	10
Not at all			Somewhat					Absolutely		

Using the scale given above, rate your degree of confidence below by recording a number from 0 to 10 in the column on the right.

Please rate how confident you are that you can:

Identify a source's mode of discourse	
Identify the type of public discourse to which a source belongs	
Manage any discomfort associated with applying truth pluralism	
Appraise a source using the correspondence theory of truth	
Appraise a source using the coherence theory of truth	

Progress Journal – Week 3

Weekly Self-Reflection

- What modes and categories of public discourse did you encounter this week (such as exposition, narration, persuasion)?
- Which tools did you apply to analyze a source in public discourse (such as applying the coherence theory of truth)?
- What insights did you gain about the situation the source was addressing?
- What difference did this insight make to a problem you needed to solve or a decision you needed to make?

Pulse-Check

0	1	2	3	4	5	6	7	8	9	10
Not at all					Somewhat					Absolutely

Using the scale given above, rate your degree of confidence below by recording a number from 0 to 10 in the column on the right.

Please rate how confident you are that you can:

Identify a source's mode of discourse	
Identify the type of public discourse to which a source belongs	
Manage any discomfort associated with applying truth pluralism	
Appraise a source using the correspondence theory of truth	
Appraise a source using the coherence theory of truth	

Progress Journal – Week 4

Final Self-Reflection and Assessment

- How has your approach to navigating public discourse changed in the past four weeks?
- How has your perception of public discourse changed in the past four weeks?
- What are two to three situations in which you feel you effectively analyzed a source in public discourse to solve a problem or make a decision?
- Describe a situation in which you could have analyzed a source in public discourse more effectively. What would you do differently?
- What skills or habits of mind do you need to enhance going forward?
- What resources and support do you need to continue to develop these skills and habits of mind?

Notes

1 Megan Gannon, "Race Is a Social Construct, Scientists Argue," *Scientific American*, February 6, 2016, https://www.scientificamerican.com/article/race-is-a-social-construct-scientists-argue/.

2 For a related discussion, see Hailey Reissman, "What Public Discourse Gets Wrong About Misinformation Online," *Research News*, Annenberg School for Communication, The University of Pennsylvania, https://www.asc.upenn.edu/news-events/news/what-public-discourse-gets-wrong-about-misinformation-online; and C. Budak, B. Nyhan, D. M. Rothschild, et al., "Misunderstanding the Harms of Online Misinformation," *Nature* 630 (2024): 45–53.

3 My go-to source for brushing up on modes of discourse is the classic, *Modern Rhetoric*. See Robert Penn Warren and Cleanth Brooks, *Modern Rhetoric* (Harcourt, Brace, Jovanovich, 4th edition, 1979).

4 Robert Penn Warren and Cleanth Brooks, *Modern Rhetoric* (Harcourt, Brace, Jovanovich, 4th edition, 1979), 56–57.

5 Robert Penn Warren and Cleanth Brooks, *Modern Rhetoric* (Harcourt, Brace, Jovanovich, 4th edition, 1979), 57.

6 Robert Penn Warren and Cleanth Brooks, *Modern Rhetoric* (Harcourt, Brace, Jovanovich, 4th edition, 1979), 57.

7 Robert Penn Warren and Cleanth Brooks, *Modern Rhetoric* (Harcourt, Brace, Jovanovich, 4th edition, 1979), 57.

8 For a more detailed description of the forms of specifically public discourse, see Michael Hannon, "Public Discourse and Its Problems," *Politics, Philosophy and Economics* 22, no. 3 (August, 2023): 336–365.

9 For more information about the increasing and intentional use of the narrative mode of discourse in news journalism see: "Storytelling and Characters in Broadcast Journalism," NBCU Academy, April 3, 2024, https://nbcuacademy.com/storytelling-characters/; Dean Pagani, "On Storytelling in Journalism," *Medium*, April 2, 2022, https://deanpagani.medium.com/on-story-telling-in-journalism-4edd7412c714; and M. Djerf-Pierre and M. Ekström, "Constructive Journalism as Practice – Storytelling in Solutions-Focused News Reporting in Mainstream News Media," *Journalism Practice* (2025): 1–19.

10 For an introduction to truth pluralism, see Nikolaj Pedersen and Cory Wright, eds., *Truth Pluralism: Current Debates* (Oxford University Press, 2012).

11 For example, in *Truth and Objectivity*, British philosopher Crispin Wright develops the concept of discourse pluralism, asserting that there is not a single characteristic of truth that crosses domains. See C. Wright, *Truth and Objectivity* (Harvard University Press, 1994). Conversely, in *Truth as One and Many*, American philosopher Michael Lynch argues that there are truth characteristics that transcend disciplines. See M. Lynch, *Truth as One and Many* (Oxford University Press, 2009).

12 There are many reasons most of us assume there is a single, absolute standard of truth. One may be the structure of our educational system. Consider changing classes in high school: students go from chemistry class, to history class, to language arts class, and no one ever suggests that each discipline employs a different conception of truth. Most of us come to assume that the conception of truth in natural sciences is the conception of truth that applies to all other fields.

13   This analogy is based on one John Horgan proposes in "Beyond the One and Only Truth," *Scientific American*, September 19, 2019, https://www.scienti ficamerican.com/blog/cross-check/pluralism-beyond-the-one-and-only-truth/. Horgan writes, "We should think like engineers, who are natural pluralists. Faced with a problem, engineers don't ask, *what is the definitive, ultimate, true solution to this problem?* That sort of thinking would be counterproductive."

14   Bertrand Russell, "Truth and Falsehood," *The Problems of Philosophy* (Oxford University Press, 13th edition, 1965), 129.

15   There are thinkers who would take issue with this statement. Some philoso-phers of mind reject the correspondence theory of truth on the grounds that our senses never convey to us an accurate perception of reality. Some cogni-tive psychologists make a similar point, asserting that cognitive biases always cloud our perception of reality. From both perspectives, because we cannot perceive real states of affairs, we cannot ever make claims that correspond to real states of affairs. I think such hard skepticism is unwarranted. I have found that, working collaboratively, people are able to correct for cognitive biases and compensate for possible shortcomings in their perceptions of reality.

16   For additional methods to address conflicting expert perspectives, see: Gustavo Sampaio A. Ribeiro, "No Need to Toss a Coin: Conflicting Scientific Expert Testimonies and Intellectual Due Process," *Law, Probability and Risk* 12, no. 4 (September–December 2013): 299–342; and Rebecca Haw, "Conflicting Expert Witnesses Can Give Inaccurate Views of Science," interviewed by Vanderbilt University School of Law, *Vanderbilt Research News*, https://news. vanderbilt.edu/2012/04/09/dueling-witnesses/; and Kristine Deroover, Simon Knight, and Tamara Bucher, "Why Do Experts Disagree? The Development of a Taxonomy," *Public Understanding of Science* 32, no. 2 (August 1, 2022): 224–246.

17   Sociologists Peter L. Berger and Thomas Luckman articulated this theory in *The Social Construction of Reality: A Treatise in the Sociology of Knowledge* (Anchor Books, 1966), building on the ideas of earlier twentieth-century social theorists such as George Herbert Meade and Emile Durkheim. See Emile Durkheim, *The Rules of Sociological Method and Selected Texts on Sociology*, edited by Steven Lukes, translated by W. D. Hall (The Free Press, 1982); and George Herbert Meade, *Mind, Self and Society from the Standpoint of a Social Behaviorist* (University of Chicago Press, 1967). Some experts would say that social constructionism posits its own theory of truth – that truth is socially constructed, even in physical sciences. Because I advise my clients based on my background in philosophy, I approach social constructionism as a subject in public discourse to which philosophical theories truth may be applied, not as itself a competing theory of truth. For a critique of social constructionism, see Ian Hacking, *The Social Construction of What?* (Harvard University Press, 1999).

18   The British philosopher and friend of Bertrand Russell, Harold Joachim, was among the first to articulate the coherence theory in *The Nature of Truth* (The Clarendon Press, 1906).

19   The British nineteenth-century thinker Thomas Carlyle first articulated this theory in his 1841 book *On Heroes, Hero-Worship and the Heroic in History*. See Thomas Carlyle, *Hero-Worship and the Heroic in History*, with an intro-duction by Michael Goldberg (University of California Press, 1993).

20   F. H. Bradley, *Essays on Truth and Reality* (Cambridge University Press, 2011).

Chapter 3

Is Forecasting Fortune-Telling?

The Limits of Moving from Specific to General

Chapter Outline

Introduction

What drives many of us to seek knowledge of the future? Discomfort with ambiguity and uncertainty? Ambition to get an advantage over others by anticipating the next "big thing"? Insurance that our biggest choices about relationships, career, finances, and family will yield the life we want for ourselves? Regret avoidance? The answer to these questions is "Yes!" To know the future is a millennia-old quest. Across time and cultures, people have employed many different methods, such as drawing cards, throwing dice, interpreting animal entrails, and identifying certain individuals as oracles, to predict the success of everything from marriages to military campaigns. All these techniques and devices purport to channel wisdom from metaphysical, spiritual sources. Today, many of us categorize such techniques as fortune-telling.

If part of what defines these techniques is reliance on a metaphysical source of information, then the types of forecasts we receive and use in our daily lives are not fortune-telling. Whether projections about the appreciation of our home, the longevity of our job, the outcome of an election, or our financial health in retirement, the forecasts we encounter are always based on data, not metaphysical perceptions.

DOI: 10.4324/9781003647034-3

The prevalence of forecasts and sophisticated forecasting techniques suggests that many of us share that millennia-old desire to know the future. How did you decide what kind of education to pursue and what kind of employment to seek? The road you take to work or for shopping – how did someone decide how many lanes it should have? How did your local government or school board determine its budget? All of these decisions involve forecasting. Young people often select a college major and a profession based on forecasts of future job markets. Departments of transportation design roads based on forecasts of future populations. Governments and institutions develop budgets based on forecasts of revenue, themselves based on projections about the number of future residents, customers, skilled employees, and students living and working in a geographical area. To meet this ongoing need to know something about the future, statisticians, scientists, and other experts have developed empirical forecasting techniques based on observation, experimentation, and mathematics.

We may seek out forecasts, for example if we meet a financial advisor; and we may be strongly encouraged to work with forecasts. Almost every organization I consult with – corporations, non-profits, government agencies – now emphasizes data-driven decision making. Through my work with individuals and groups in diverse roles in these organizations, I have observed that even astute, well-informed professionals can misinterpret forecasts. In essence, people tend to be overconfident in them. There are several reasons for this overconfidence.[1]

In some cases, I see clients too readily accept forecasts that they see as positive and beneficial for themselves, for example a university dean who unquestioningly accepts rosy predictions about the number of students who will accept their admissions offers and pay full tuition fees to the university. In other cases, the credibility a client attributes to the source of a forecast leads to overconfidence in positive predictions and underestimation of uncertainty. Sometimes, a client may not fully understand a forecast, but they are embarrassed to say so, which leads to unquestioning acceptance. In other words, people often attribute to forecasts – *because* they are based on data from credible sources – a degree of predictive power the forecasts do not possess. Even savvy, highly educated professionals can assume a forecast provides certainty, when it actually provides a way of navigating uncertainty. The need to *know*, to be certain, can lead any of us to oversimplify and misinterpret the information on which we base decisions. In striving to make the right decision, any of us, ironically, can make a poorly informed, ineffective decision.

In the previous chapter, we explored theories of truth as a way of accurately understanding the information and recommendations we receive through public discourse – broadcast news, print media, social media. In this chapter, I offer an approach to interpreting accurately the information and advice we receive in the form of forecasts. To begin, I will consider with you some common types of forecasts we may all consult. Next, I will share some insights about interpreting forecasts I have gained through experiences with clients. Third, I will invite you to consider the fundamental limitation of forecasting, not addressed by most experts: the problem of induction. The problem of induction is that speculating about unobserved things based on things that we have observed does not give certainty about those unobserved things; rather, it provides probabilities about them. My clients have found awareness of induction's limitations particularly useful for better-informed decision making. Fourth, I will propose thinking in terms of probabilities as a way to navigate the limitations of induction. Finally, I will offer you tools I have used with my clients, to help you more accurately assess forecasts in your professional and personal life.

Everyday Forecasts

The year 2007 – not the best year to buy a house, but the year I purchased my current home. At the time, I accepted, with few reservations, forecasts about home values increasing significantly in the near term. I doubted the value of a property could increase dramatically forever. Yet, I never expected property would actually *decrease* in value. Many properties, including mine, did lose value between 2007 and 2009. My experience, shared by many other people, illustrates one of the everyday situations in which we turn to expertly developed forecasts: understanding the value of our homes (and other real estate we may own).

Fast forward from the housing crash of 2007. A daily ritual for many people today is checking automated valuation model (AVM) websites, such as Zillo.com and Realtor.com regarding the value of a home.[2] These sites forecast the value of specific properties based on a combination of data, such as tax records and multiple listing services used by real estate agents. By checking these sites, we get a forecast of what our property could sell for (and this helps us estimate other things, such as our net worth).

Typically, we want to understand more than the projected value of a specific property. Unless you need to sell because you have to move immediately, you usually want to answer the question, "When is the best time to sell to maximize my investment?" Answering this question involves looking at forecasts about home values in your area and across the country.[3] You may research housing trends and find that the historical pattern of real estate values in the United States indicates residential real estate appreciates at an average rate of 5 percent per year.[4] To get more precise data regarding the right time to sell your home, you may investigate forecasts of new home construction. You want to find out: Will new homes be built soon, increasing housing stock, driving prices down, indicating I should sell now? Or: Is new construction slow, possibly decreasing the stock of houses for sale, driving prices up, indicating I should wait to sell?

That many of us consult real estate forecasts daily to answer questions such as these leads to consideration of another type of forecast-based advice we seek: retirement planning. For many of us, deciding when and if to sell our home is part of retirement planning. In addition, you may also consult with a certified financial planner or similar professional regarding your readiness for retirement. These conversations often involve an assessment of your financial fitness for retirement. A financial advisor might forecast that you will easily afford your needs and wants in retirement. Or, they may advise you that you are in a more precarious position, meaning you may not be able to retire fully, or that you may experience reduced circumstances in retirement. If your retirement income looks like it will not pay for your needs and wants, an advisor may recommend ways you could invest and increase your retirement income. Although a financial advisor may not start a conversation by sharing details about the methods they use to make such forecasts, you provide them the sources of data they draw on: your current assets and debts and your future sources of income (revenue from real estate sold, pension payments, Social Security payments, dividends from investments).

In addition to these forecasts that we routinely encounter in our personal lives, many of us encounter forecasts in our work life. If, for instance, you work for a cultural institution, such as a museum or library, you might receive forecasts about the number of people graduating from professional schools over a specific period who could become visitors and donors to your institution. If you work for a company that manufactures consumer products or business-to-business products, you will receive forecasts about your consumers' demand for your product. Demand forecasts can inform sales forecasts, which can inform marketing strategies. Whether you work in the corporate or non-profit sectors, you may consult economic forecasts for insights about how much money consumers have to spend on goods, services, and philanthropy. Whether you are a small business owner, work for a multinational corporation, or a government agency, you may seek forecasts about future employees. As current employees retire, you need to anticipate the quantity of people entering the workforce with the education and skills your organization needs.

Clients Seeking Certainty

The sources of data for these various types of forecasts can be easy to identify. As mentioned, real estate forecasts can use publicly accessible tax assessments and licenses for new construction, and multiple listing services showing homes for sale at a given time. You may realize, however, that knowing the sources of data does not answer all your questions about how experts develop different types of forecasts. You may be like Lisa, an open-minded, curious executive I coached, who sought a deeper understanding of forecasting methods. As her company made generous provisions for her retirement, Lisa decided to work with a financial planner. After analyzing her financial information, the planner whom Lisa selected declared that Lisa was in the "safe" zone for a secure retirement. (The planner defined the "safe" zone as maintaining 90 percent of peak earned income in retirement.)

According to Lisa, her planner arrived at her diagnosis by plugging information into proprietary algorithms used to simulate different scenarios that could impact Lisa's financial future. Still, Lisa wanted to know more about the reasoning process behind the diagnosis that she was financially "safe" for retirement. I guided Lisa in researching methods forecasters often use. We started an internet search with the question, "How does financial modeling work?" This was prior to the prevalence of AI, so we quickly found several useful, credible explanations from specific sources. A *Harvard Business Review* article, "How to Choose the Right Forecasting Technique," seemed like a good starting point.[5] The article provided an overview of three forecasting methods most often used in business: qualitative techniques, time series analysis and projection, and causal models.

The article explained that qualitative data, such as interviews with clients and consumers, and literature reviews of scholarly research may not take the past into consideration. In contrast, time series analysis and projection rely entirely on historical data, focusing on patterns. The article further explained that causal models examine relationships between different elements in a system (such as a production process), and that causal models also rely on historical data. This article mentions regression analysis as a particularly useful approach to developing a causal model. Lisa wanted to move on to another *Harvard Business Review* article, "A Refresher on Regression Analysis," by Amy Galo.[6]

Galo explained regression analysis with an accessible example, involving a sales manager trying to predict the upcoming month's sales figures. The sales manager knows that multiple factors can impact the rate of sales. Regression analysis mathematically distills which of those factors actually has an impact on sales.[7] Galo further noted that factors potentially impacting next month's sales are understood as variables in regression analysis. Regression analysis involves two variables: the dependent variable, which is the main factor you want to predict or understand (monthly sales in the example); and independent variables, which are the factors likely influencing the dependent variable.[8] Galo offered a note of caution: regression and other types of analysis that seek to explain relationships among variables can show correlations among variables. But correlations do not necessarily indicate cause-effect relationships. For instance, a regression may show there is a correlation between weather events and monthly sales – sales are higher on stormy days. However, this does not necessarily mean that stormy days cause the increase in sales. There might be another variable impacting sales that you have yet not identified.[9]

Lisa was familiar with the adage "correlation is not causation." For Lisa, Galo's article offered a helpful reminder that, if you cannot identify a cause-effect relationship among variables, finding a correlation may not tell you anything. Lisa noticed that in describing regression analysis and its possible pitfalls, Galo referred to hypothesis testing. For Lisa, hypothesis testing was a new concept. My search with Lisa took us to another expert source, "A Beginner's Guide to Hypothesis Testing in Business," an article written by Tim Stobierski, published by Harvard Business School.[10]

Stobierski explained that, when used in statistical analysis, a hypothesis offers a possible cause-effect explanation about the relationship between variables. Typically, a researcher formulates a hypothesis as an if-then statement, such as, if x happens, then y will happen.[11] Stobierski further noted that statistical hypothesis tests typically draw on sample data to extrapolate insights about the whole, of which the sample is a part. The business goal of hypothesis testing is to equip professionals to prove or disprove their theories and assumptions before acting on them.[12]

Stobierski's article helped Lisa realize more questions about hypothesis testing, so we visited a website designed to prepare financial professionals to complete the Canadian Securities Course exam (a credential required to practice as a securities broker in Canada). We looked at the section "Quantitative Methods in Finance: Hypothesis Testing in Financial Analysis." The site uses an illustration with which a financial planner such as Lisa's might be familiar. The illustration involves an analyst who wants to investigate whether or not a new investment strategy will yield returns greater than the market average. The investigation involves conducting a statistical experiment, comparing observed data against what a specific hypothesis predicts.[13] The analyst uses hypothesis testing to ascertain whether there is enough statistical evidence in a data sample to infer that a specific condition is true for the entire group of which the sample is a part.[14] Such a hypothesis test for an investment strategy would involve at least two hypotheses:

The alternative hypothesis: The proposed strategy's average return is greater than the market's average return.

The null hypothesis: The proposed strategy's average return is equal to the market's average return (in other words, the alternative hypothesis is disproven).

The entry wraps up by summarizing methodological errors that may complicate the process of proving or disproving the alternative hypotheses.[15]

After consulting these "meta-expert" sources, Lisa felt confident that she was, as her financial planner asserted, in the "safe" zone for retirement. Lisa observed that the methods she discovered involved the scientific process of developing, then proving or disproving hypotheses. She noted that the methods employed critical thinking skills, such distinguishing correlation and causation. The methods also involved mathematical calculations, which are objective, not subjective matters of perspective and opinion. Lisa was satisfied that the conclusions resulting from statistical methods, like those used by her financial planner, rest on careful analysis of data, not guesses.

Lisa's story illustrates why many astute, reflective people perceive forecasts as expressing certainties, and are thus overconfident in them. Most of us perceive science and math as sources of certainties, such as the law of gravity and $2 + 2 = 4$. Consequently, assertions, such as forecasts, that are mathematically derived using a scientific approach may seem indisputable. In the case of the conclusion "You are in the safe zone for retirement," this quality of undeniability is very appealing. Likewise, in a situation like the sales manager's example offered by Galo, a forecast's quality of undeniability is similarly reassuring. If a sales manager receives a data-based conclusion, such as that the variable impacting sales in winter months has been identified, the sales manager can determine how to address or manipulate the variable, and thus have an apparently foolproof way to increase sales.

Expert sources themselves may convey the sense that their conclusions are certain, incontrovertible; the outcomes they predict inevitable. Consider a situation involving another executive I coached, Elliott. Elliott sought a vendor to consult regarding a marketing plan. Elliott was very impressed by a particular vendor, and we reviewed their website together.[16] The vendor's website indicated that their methods for developing client websites are based on behavioral science experiments.

The vendor offered the assurance that applied behavioral science enables clients to deploy solutions that are backed by scientific evidence, so that clients can see exactly why their last idea influenced decision making, and can quantify the effect of their ideas on human behavior. The vendor's website further explained that there are predictable patterns in individuals' irrationality, which can be used to design frameworks that help people make better decisions. Based on this, the vendor indicated that they offer tested and verified solutions, developed by behavioral scientists, which create choice architectures to guide people to the right decisions.

To Elliott, the vendor's statements sounded definitive: using their tools, Elliott could be certain that people who visited his firm's website would be influenced into purchasing what his firm wanted them to purchase. (The behavioral science experiments the vendor referred to employ some of the hypothesis-testing techniques also employed in forecasting. Chapter 4 involves a more careful examination of the claims of behavioral science). Clearly, a website advertising expert services differs from articles published by a highly respected business school. That a consulting service wants to convey a sense of certainty about the results their products will produce is perhaps to be expected. (Hence, a purpose of this chapter is to equip you to interpret the claims of such websites more accurately.)

In contrast, the expert advice Lisa discovered presented a more thorough description of the statistical methods used to develop forecasts, including the possible pitfalls and errors to which various techniques are prone. While providing this broad perspective, the expert sources Lisa reviewed *did not provide all the information you need accurately to understand forecasts*. Ironically, Lisa's research contributed to her confidence in her planner's forecast, rather than helping her assess the forecast more critically. No forecast can give certainty. The reason is not simply that practitioners can make mistakes in their computations or construction of hypotheses. The reason involves the basic logic underlying all forecasts. Understanding this logic, and its inherent limits, is key to accurately understanding forecasts, rather than being overconfident in the futures they project.

Demystifying the Logic of Forecasts

All the sources I shared in the story about Lisa explain that forecasting techniques involve drawing inferences from features in a sample of data to reach a broader conclusion. The type of data sampled can vary. It can be a sample of previous events used to predict a future event, as in time-series analysis. It can be a sample of people assumed to represent a broader population, used to predict the preferences and decisions of that broader population, as in causal models. This move, from sample to generalization is called *induction*.

I learned by working with Lisa, Elliott, and other talented people that demystifying the logic underlying forecasts – induction – is an effective antidote to overconfidence in specific forecasts. One way to demystify inductive reasoning is to recognize where we use induction in much of our everyday decision making. To illustrate, suppose I have observed that, if I arrive at my favorite take-out buffet after 5:00 pm, most of the food will have gone, because people who do not work 9:00–5:00 were able to get their food earlier. I conclude that I should arrive by 4:30, and that if I cannot arrive by 4:30, I should go elsewhere for dinner.

This example illustrates everyday inductive reasoning. I do not *know* that on a given day, little food will remain after 5:00 pm. But, based on previous experience, it seems probable that on any given day, little food will remain after 5:00, and it will save me time and frustration if I plan accordingly. In other words, valid inductive reasoning provides good but not conclusive grounds for the acceptance of a conclusion.[17] Forecasts work in the same way: they can provide good but not conclusive grounds for expecting a particular future state, such as "You will be safe in retirement." Acting on a probable conclusion always involves some risk. Using the take-out buffet example, if I forego the take-out buffet because I will get there after 5:00, and it turns out today there is plenty of food after 5:00, I might miss out on some enjoyable entree for dinner. The risk of finding little food, however, is greater than the risk of missing an enjoyable entree, so I feel safer choosing a different place for dinner. In a similar way, forecasts can inform more consequential decision making, although they cannot eliminate uncertainty and risk.

We can consider my simple example of deciding where to buy dinner, or a more complex example, say, of collecting sales figures from the past eight Novembers to predict sales for this coming November. Both these examples illustrate a logical process called induction by enumeration. Induction by enumeration is foundational to forecasting. This type of induction involves inferring from the fact that "All As observed so far are Bs" to the conclusion "All As whatsoever are Bs" or the opposite, "No As observed so far are Bs, therefore no As whatsoever are Bs."[18] To illustrate further, suppose a pollster conducts a survey of members of the House of Representatives and 100 members respond. All 100 respondents indicate they have used their official letterheads for personal correspondence. Using induction by enumeration, the pollster might predict from this data that all members of the House of Representatives will at some point use their official letterheads for personal correspondence.

Building on induction by enumeration, the amount in a sample may be used to describe the occurrence of an event or characteristic. Consider our current example. There are 435 members of the House of Representatives. The pollster can represent this sample of one hundred members as 23 percent of the House of Representatives. Using a version of induction by enumeration, statistical induction, the pollster could state that 23 percent of all House members use their official letterheads for personal correspondence.[19] A related step, proportional induction, is inferring from the frequency of a characteristic's occurrence in a sample to the frequency of that characteristic's occurrence in the parent population.[20] In our survey of House members example, the researcher conducting the survey could conclude that typically 23 percent of House members use their official letterheads for personal correspondence. You can see how these steps play a role in forecasting. Using induction by enumeration, and statistical and proportional induction, a researcher could use a survey to forecast that citizens can expect 23 percent of members of the House of Representatives to use their official letterhead for personal correspondence.

Realizing where they routinely used induction helped Lisa, Elliott, and other clients contextualize forecasts more effectively. A greater insight for clients has been to recognize a fundamental limitation of induction itself: we cannot *know* unobserved things based on what we know of observed things. Induction is the foundational logic of forecasting. Thus, all forecasts are subject to the limitation of induction.[21] One of the sources discussed in Lisa's story, "How to Choose the Right Forecasting Technique," hints as this limitation, observing that statistical techniques all assume current patterns will continue into the future. The odds of this assumption being correct are greater over the short term than the long term.[22] Because of the limitation of induction, however, even in the short term, forecasts do not present certain outcomes. That the future looks like the past, that a whole population looks like its sample, are always assumptions in inductive reasoning, which could be disproven at any time by unforeseen, not previously experienced phenomena.

The Scottish eighteenth-century philosopher David Hume was the first to articulate the inherent limitation in the move from "observed As are Bs" to "all As whatsoever are Bs." Hume addressed conceptual issues emerging from the growth of science and the scientific method. In the years since Hume wrote, techniques such as observation, hypothesis creation, and experimentation have become even more prevalent. Thus, his observations continue to be relevant. Hume recognized that people *assume* the future will resemble the past, although the only evidence we have for this assumption is that in most of our lived experience, the future generally follows past patterns (for example, crops wither without a certain amount of water; tides ebb and flow at regular intervals).

Famously, Hume used our experience of a candle's flame to illustrate the assumption embedded in induction. He observed that everyone remembers seeing a type of object, a flame, and at the same time feeling a type of sensation, heat. He noted that whenever we see a particular flame, we remember the constant conjunction of flames and heat in all past instances.[23] Hume generalized that, in most of our daily experiences, we remember frequent instances of specific types of objects, and also that other specific types of objects always attend them.[24] Hume concluded that we identify the first type of object as a cause and the other as an effect, and infer the existence of the one from that of the other.[25] Hume suggested that the inference from cause to effect is actually an assumption we continually make. It is not a fact we can ultimately prove.[26] In other words, induction rests upon a continual *assumption* that the future will resemble the past, that a sample will resemble a whole. Hume asserted that induction is thus always inconclusive. Many philosophers since Hume have proposed ways to compensate for this inconclusiveness, which we will explore shortly.[27] Identifying this assumption that underlies all forecasting has helped my clients more accurately assess forecasts, avoid overconfidence, and make more informed personal and professional decisions.

The Limitation of Induction in Machine Learning and Data Science

A senior leader asked me to review an AI training curriculum his organization developed, to introduce employees to the firm's custom-developed AI tools. I found the curriculum well designed, focusing on the ways different functions and roles should use various AI tools. My client and I agreed, however, that something was missing: there was no content related to assessing critically the data provided by machine learning.

Our realization about the gap in the training highlights the importance of identifying all of the contexts in which we need to recognize the limitations in induction. Although the two client stories in this chapter highlight the use of induction in financial forecasts and predicting consumer behavior, understanding the problem of induction is relevant to any context involving samples of data used to make predictions.

Data science and machine learning both rely on induction to identify patterns in data and make predictions. For example, machine learning uses algorithms to learn from specific examples in order to make predictions about new, uncollected data. This predictive capacity allows a model to make decisions, so that it does not have to be explicitly programmed for every possible scenario.[28] Likewise, specialties within data science, such as predictive analytics, use historical data to forecast future outcomes. In other words, both machine learning and predictive analytics involve the inductive move from "observed As are Bs," to "all As must be Bs."

As with forecasting, Bayesian methods of determining probabilities can help make predictions more precise, but no prediction is certain. Thus, when you receive information generated by machine learning, or data science techniques, you should exercise the same prudence recommended in this chapter regarding forecasts. The toolkit at the end of this chapter can help you assess not only forecasts, but any conclusions based on predictions and induction.

Overcorrecting for Overconfidence

When I first discussed the limitation of induction with Lisa, she exclaimed, "You mean I shouldn't believe my financial planner? I'm not safe in retirement?" Similarly, upon understanding the limitation of induction, Elliott wanted to adopt a doubt-till-proven-true skepticism about forecasts. I replied that understanding a forecast is more subtle than either "It's true, accept it unconditionally," or "It's false, you cannot trust it." Well-researched forecasts are not black or white; rather, they present a range of grays. They incorporate the likelihoods of specific outcomes in specific conditions. I encouraged Lisa and Elliott to develop a position of neutrality, rather than overcompensate for overconfidence with a strong skepticism about forecasts. Lisa came to recognize that her financial planner was really saying "You are more likely to be safe in retirement than you are to be financially insecure in retirement." This refined understanding enabled Lisa to assess her financial position in an ongoing way, for example, weighing the pros and cons of downsizing her home at a particular time, the viability of changing jobs at a particular age, and of retiring at different ages.

To help Lisa, Elliott, and other clients avoid overcorrecting for their overconfidence in forecasts, I explored with them the role probabilities play in forecasting. Determining the probability of specific outcomes is a way to compensate for the fundamental limitation of induction. Some induction-based conclusions can be more likely than others. There are theoretical debates among mathematicians and philosophers about the most accurate method to determine probability: Frequentist or Bayesian.[29] However, picking a side in such debates is not necessary. Simply identifying how each method determines the probability of specific outcomes can enhance your ability to access forecasts.

The Frequentist approach defines probability as the long-term frequency of an event occurring. In other words, the probability of a certain event is the number of times that event occurs over the course of many repetitions. For example, imagine a soup company offers 25 percent off its cans of soup every July for ten years, to boost sales in warm months. For five of the Julys, soup sales increase and for five of them soup sales stay the same. Based on this, you could forecast there is a 50 percent chance the company can increase soup sales any July by cutting the price by a quarter.

The Bayesian approach (named after eighteenth-century English mathematician, philosopher, and minister Thomas Bayes, a contemporary of Hume) incorporates existing (sometime called prior) knowledge about a type of event in making predictions about the occurrence of that type of event. The Bayesian approach also involves updating the prediction based on new evidence. For example, suppose a friend tells you about a marketing campaign that significantly increased sales for their company. This interests you in trying a similar type of campaign at your company. Your friend's experience represents prior knowledge, which you draw on to predict the success of your company's use of a similar type of campaign. Suppose further you launch a campaign like that used by your friend, and after a week, you check sales figures. The sales figures represent knowledge you can use to update your prediction about the campaign's effectiveness.

Lisa and Elliott found that their awareness of the different techniques used to determine probability helped them maintain a balanced perception of forecasts. On the one hand, realizing that there are different techniques that may produce different results helped them offset overconfidence. On the other hand, understanding that determining probability can compensate for the limitations of induction enabled them to recognize insights forecasts can offer. Maintaining a neutral perception of forecasts is crucial. Otherwise, you are in danger of either arbitrarily rejecting useful information or of underestimating uncertainty, overlooking potential risks, and making decisions based on unrealistic expectations.

While recognizing there are different methods to determine probability can enable you to offset overconfidence in forecasts, ideally, the same methods, applied to the same data by many different people, result in the same conclusion. This process: different people, at different times and in different places, using the same data and methods to arrive at the same conclusion is replication. Replication is another way to compensate for the limitation of induction. For instance, the economics experiment "the ultimatum game" has been replicated multiple times.[30] Across different cultures and populations, researchers consistently observe that people often reject unfair offers in a simple decision-making scenario, preferring fairness even when it means foregoing personal gain. The more often an outcome is reproduced is different contexts, the stronger the inductive inference, which in this example is the move from "observed people prioritize fairness in certain contexts" to "most people would prioritize fairness in those contexts."

A forecast that is similarly replicable is thus more trustworthy than a forecast that has not been replicated. Asking whether or not a forecast has been replicated is increasingly important. Several fields employing statistical research, including finance, may face a "replication crisis," meaning the findings of a particular researcher cannot be reproduced by other researchers using the same methods and data.[31] Nonetheless, the best practices of forecasting include replicating results.[32] Results that have not been replicated are not phony, but they are not as trustworthy as replicated results for decision making.

Recognizing how probability and replication can compensate for the limitations of induction has helped my clients, such as Lisa and Elliott, better assess forecasts in their personal and professional lives. Likewise, recognizing where they use inductive reasoning every day, as well as recognizing the fundamental limitation of induction, has helped my clients demystify forecasts, and thus avoid overconfidence in them. Based on my work in coaching executives, as well as teaching critical thinking seminars in many contexts (biomedical technology, aerospace, and financial technology to name a few), I offer you the following tools to enhance your ability to assess forecasts with equilibrium, balancing confidence and doubt.

Toolkit for Accurately Assessing Forecasts

Tool 1: Enhance Uncertainty Tolerance

Given that a primary motivation for seeking forecasts is reducing uncertainty, increasing your tolerance for uncertainty is fundamental to managing overconfidence in forecasts. Uncertainty tolerance involves our cognitive and emotional responses to indeterminacy. Experiencing uncertainty can produce negative emotions, such as anxiety. Such anxiety or stress does not mean you are unable successfully to navigate uncertainty. Several techniques can help you increase your uncertainty tolerance.[33] First, recognize that being uncertain is not a failing. It does not undermine your credibility. Second, identify your areas of adaptive expertise: your core knowledge and core skills that can be applied in different situations where there is uncertainty. Third, identify what is under your control that can reduce uncertainty (your knowledge and experience, interactions with peers, and sense of purpose).

Tool 2: Leverage Hypothetical Thinking

All of us have at some point mused, "hypothetically, what if ..." when considering a possible course of action. Hypothetical thinking is using our imagination to simulate possible results of a decision. Envision and explore possible scenarios that could result from acting on, and not acting on a forecast. Using your imagination to simulate possible outcomes from acting on a particular forecast will help you maintain a neutral perspective regarding a forecast, neither overconfident, nor dismissively skeptical. Hypothetical thinking can be especially useful for remaining realistic about a forecast that seems to offer particularly positive results for you.

Tool 3: Practice Counterfactual Thinking

From a philosophical perspective, counterfactual thinking involves using imagination in a way that is similar to hypothetical thinking. Without naming it as such, we practice counterfactual thinking from an early age. Imagine youngsters on a playground near a building. One youngster suggests practicing baseball near the building. Another youngster responds, "What if I miss the ball and it breaks a window?" The second youngster's response is counterfactual: a potential fact that undercuts the proposal of practicing baseball near windows.

A conversation between two of my clients provides another illustration. One client was adamant that higher employee morale causes greater productivity. The other client countered that when people are afraid of being laid off in a recession, they are more productive. The second client offers a counterfactual, a piece of information that could disprove the first client's assertion. Perhaps the counterfactual claim – people are more productive when they are afraid – is mistaken. Finding evidence to *prove* it is mistaken strengthens the validity of the assertion "Higher employee morale causes greater productivity." If you can identify what would disprove a conclusion, and overcome this possible disconfirming evidence, you can be more confident the conclusion is correct.

While we may learn this skill with school friends, in adulthood it also often involves deliberately seeking points of view from people who differ from ourselves. Discuss forecasts with friends or colleagues who have a background, an education, or a perspective different from yours. Their responses can facilitate counterfactual thinking, helping you better appraise a forecast's quality and relevance for you.

Tool 4: Harness Probability Judgments

Like hypothetical and counterfactual thinking, we make probability judgments as we go through our daily routines. We may start a workday asking ourselves: What is the likelihood I will get to work fastest on the interstate versus surface streets? What is the likelihood my flight will be delayed, making an earlier flight more prudent? When we answer questions such as these, we make probability judgments.

Embrace this capacity and use it more intentionally. Consider that future scenarios are possible, some may be probable, but none are foregone conclusions. For example, think of possible future outcomes on a spectrum from good to bad – ranging from what you want to achieve to what you want to avoid – not simply good *or* bad. Be aware of and avoid other types of binary thinking that can cloud your assessment of a forecast. Binary thinking can include adages such as, "If it can go wrong, it will go wrong" and "Lightning doesn't strike twice in the same place." In reality, one negative event does not categorically rule out the immediate occurrence of another negative event. Similarly, all possible negative events are not equally likely to occur.

Tool 5: Pursue Replication

Seeking second and third points of view is a way you can practice replication. This can compensate for the fact that a specific forecast may not yet have been replicated. Many of us will seek a second medical opinion upon receiving a diagnosis from a particular physician. Approach forecasts in a similar way. Where possible, seek forecasts from multiple sources. For example, seek a diagnosis of your fitness for retirement from several financial planners, and look for alignment in their answers.

Tool 6: Question Forecasts Confidently

A goal of this chapter is to empower you, so that you can avoid being mystified or intimidated by mathematical and scientific techniques used in forecasting. In some ways, the computations involved in forecasts are not as important the ways those computations are used. Key questions to ask about any forecast are:

- On what data is the forecast based?
- On what assumptions is the forecast based?
- How often is the forecast updated?
- Will the forecast be monitored and adjusted based on new information?

Trustworthy forecasts use updated assumptions and are adjusted regularly to align with new data.

Progress Journal

You can sustain changes in your thinking in a similar way to the way you might change habits, such as what you eat and how much you exercise. Track your progress by keeping a journal of how you implement new ideas, noting which are easy to apply and where you run into challenges.

Progress Journal – Week 1

Weekly Self-Reflection

- What forecasts did you encounter this week (work-related, personal finance-related, other)?
- Which tools did you apply to the situation (for example, probability judgments, counterfactual thinking)?
- What questions did you ask to contextualize and better understand the forecast?
- What insights did you gain about the situation the forecast is intended to inform?

Pulse-Check

0	1	2	3	4	5	6	7	8	9	10
Not at all					Somewhat					Absolutely

Using the scale given above, rate your degree of confidence below by recording a number from 0 to 10 in the column on the right.

Please rate how confident you are that you can:

Look for data or expert opinion to replicate a forecast	
Ask clarifying questions of the person or group making the forecast	
Manage any negative emotions related to experiencing uncertainty	
Seek disconfirming information to test a conclusion	
Identify where a specific forecast uses induction to arrive at a conclusion	

Progress Journal – Week 2

Weekly Self-Reflection

- What forecasts did you encounter this week (work-related, personal finance-related, other)?
- Which tools did you apply to the situation (for example, probability judgments, counterfactual thinking)?
- What questions did you ask to contextualize and better understand the forecast?
- What insights did you gain about the situation the forecast is intended to inform?

Pulse-Check

0	1	2	3	4	5	6	7	8	9	10
Not at all					Somewhat					Absolutely

Using the scale given above, rate your degree of confidence below by recording a number from 0 to 10 in the column on the right.

Please rate how confident you are that you can:

Look for data or expert opinion to replicate a forecast	
Ask clarifying questions of the person or group making the forecast	
Manage any negative emotions related to experiencing uncertainty	
Seek disconfirming information to test a conclusion	
Identify where a specific forecast uses induction to arrive at a conclusion	

Progress Journal – Week 3

Weekly Self-Reflection

- What forecasts did you encounter this week (work-related, personal finance-related, other)?
- Which tools did you apply to the situation (for example, probability judgments, counterfactual thinking)?
- What questions did you ask to contextualize and better understand the forecast?
- What insights did you gain about the situation the forecast is intended to inform?

Pulse-Check

0	1	2	3	4	5	6	7	8	9	10
Not at all				Somewhat					Absolutely	

Using the scale given above, rate your degree of confidence below by recording a number from 0 to 10 in the column on the right.

Please rate how certain you are that you can:

Look for data or expert opinion to replicate a forecast	
Ask clarifying questions of the person or group making the forecast	
Manage any negative emotions related to experiencing uncertainty	
Seek disconfirming information to test a conclusion	
Identify where a specific forecast uses induction to arrive at a conclusion	

Progress Journal – Week 4

Final Self-Reflection and Assessment

- How has your approach to interpreting forecasts changed in the past four weeks?
- How has your perception of forecasts changed in the past four weeks?
- What are two to three situations in which you feel you used forecasts effectively to solve a problem or make a decision?
- Describe a situation in which you could have used forecasts more effectively. What would you do differently?
- What skills or habits of mind do you need to enhance going forward?
- What resources and support do you need to continue to develop skills?

Notes

1 Overconfidence in forecasts is well documented. See, for example, Richard H. Thaler, "The Overconfidence Problem in Forecasting," *The New York Times*, August 21, 2010; Paul Saffo, "Six Rules for Effective Forecasting," *Harvard Business Review*, July, 2007; Baruch Fischhoff, "What Forecasts (Seem to) Mean," *International Journal of Forecasting* 10 (1994): 387–403.

2 James Rodriguez, "Zillow's Price Estimates Are Screwing up Homebuying," *Yahoo Finance Business Insider*, December 18, 2024, https://www.msn.com/en-us/money/realestate/ar-AA1w4xFn.

3 John Meszanos, "A Brief Review of House Price Forecasting Methods," *The Counselors of Real Estate* 48, no. 4 (February 7, 2024), https://cre.org.real-est ate-issues/a-brief-review-of-house-price-forecasting-methods/.

4 Freddie Mac House Price Index Price Appreciation 1990–2023, Statista.com, https://www.statista.com/statistics/275159/freddie-mac-house-price-index-from-2009/.

5 John C. Chamber, Satinder K. Mullik, and Donald D. Smith, "How to Choose the Right Forecasting Technique," *Harvard Business Review*, 1971.

6 Amy Galo, "A Refresher on Regression Analysis," *Harvard Business Review*, November 4, 2015.

7 Amy Galo, "A Refresher on Regression Analysis," *Harvard Business Review*, November 4, 2015.

8 Amy Galo, "A Refresher on Regression Analysis," *Harvard Business Review*, November 4, 2015.

9 Amy Galo, "A Refresher on Regression Analysis," *Harvard Business Review*, November 4, 2015.

10 Tim Stobierski, "A Beginner's Guide to Hypothesis Testing," Harvard Business School, Business Insights Blog, March 30, 2021, https://online.hbs.edu/blog/post/hypothesis-testing.

11 Tim Stobierski, "A Beginner's Guide to Hypothesis Testing," Harvard Business School, Business Insights Blog, March 30, 2021, https://online.hbs.edu/blog/post/hypothesis-testing.

12 Tim Stobierski, "A Beginner's Guide to Hypothesis Testing," Harvard Business School, Business Insights Blog, March 30, 2021, https://online.hbs.edu/blog/post/hypothesis-testing.

13 Canadian Securities Institute, "Study Tools," January, 2025, https://www.csi.ca/en/learning/courses/csc/study-tools.

14 Canadian Securities Institute, "Study Tools," January, 2025, https://www.csi.ca/en/learning/courses/csc/study-tools.

15 Canadian Securities Institute, "Study Tools," January, 2025, https://www.csi.ca/en/learning/courses/csc/study-tools.

16 My client was considering the website of Optimizely. Website accessed December 31, 2024, https://www.optimizely.com/optimization-glossary/beh avioral-science/.

17 Howard Kahane, *Logic and Contemporary Rhetoric: The Use of Reasoning in Everyday Life* (University of Kansas Press, 2017), 221.

18 Howard Kahane, *Logic and Contemporary Rhetoric: The Use of Reasoning in Everyday Life* (University of Kansas Press, 2017).

19 Howard Kahane, *Logic and Contemporary Rhetoric: The Use of Reasoning in Everyday Life* (University of Kansas Press, 2017), 224.

20 Max Black, "Induction," *The Encyclopedia of Philosophy*, ed. Paul Edwards (Macmillan and The Free Press, 1967): 169–180.
21 Enriqueta Aragones, Itzhak Gilboa, Andrew Postlewaite, and David Schmeidler, "From Cases to Rules: Induction and Regression," University of Pennsylvania School of Arts and Sciences, April, 2002, https://www.sas.upenn.edu/~apost lew/paper/pdf/AGPS_From_Cases_to_Rules.pdf.
22 John C. Chamber, Satinder K. Mullik, and Donald D. Smith, "How to Choose the Right Forecasting Technique," *Harvard Business Review*, 1971.
23 David Hume, *A Treatise of Human Nature*, eds. David Fate Norton and Mary J. Norton (Oxford University Press, 2000).
24 David Hume, *A Treatise of Human Nature* (Book 1, part iii, section 6), eds. David Fate Norton and Mary J. Norton (Oxford University Press, 2000).
25 David Hume, *A Treatise of Human Nature*, eds. David Fate Norton and Mary J. Norton (Oxford University Press, 2000).
26 David Hume, *A Treatise of Human Nature*, eds. David Fate Norton and Mary J. Norton (Oxford University Press, 2000).
27 David Hume, *A Treatise of Human Nature*, eds. David Fate Norton and Mary J. Norton (Oxford University Press, 2000). Later philosophers, such as scientist and mathematician Charles S. Pierce, have asserted that induction, particularly in the natural sciences, can lead to knowledge in the form of "laws" – descriptive generalizations about the ways some aspects of the natural world behave in specific circumstances. See Charles S. Pierce, *Illustrations in the Logic of Science*, 5.145., ed. Cornelis de Waal (Open Court Publishing Company, 2014). Induction works less well in producing descriptive generalizations when applied to human behavior. The challenges of applying methods from natural sciences to human behavior are explored in Chapter 4. Analytic philosopher Nelson Goodman articulates a famous reframing of Hume's problem, suggesting we can identify which characteristics of a given object or situation are "projectible" – meaning that we can reasonably infer their continued presence based on past observations. See Nelson Goodman, *Fact, Fiction Forecast* (Harvard University Press, 1983).
28 For a more detailed discussion of induction's role in various types of AI, see Thomas M. Powers and Jean-Gabriel Ganascia, "The Ethics of AI," *The Oxford Handbook of Ethics of AI*, eds. Marcus D. Dubber, Frank Pasquale, and Sunit Das (Oxford University Press, 2020), 26–51.
29 Aubrey Clayton, *Bernoulli's Fallacy: Statistical Illogic and the Crisis of Modern Science* (Cambridge University Press, 2021); Christian Keysers, Valeria Gazzola, and Eric-Jan Wagonmakers, "Using Bayes Factor Hypothesis Testing in Neuroscience to Establish Evidence of Absence," *National Neuroscience* 23, no. 7 (June 29, 2020): 788–799, https://pubmed.ncbi.nlm.nih.gov/32601 411/#:~:text=Abstract,the%20absence%20of%20an%20effect; Deborah G. Mayo, *Statistical Inference as Severe Testing: How to Get Beyond the Statistics Wars* (Cambridge University Press, 2018); Eric-Jan Wagenmakers, Michael Lee, Geoff Iverson, et al., "Bayesian Versus Frequentist Inference," *Bayesian Evaluation of Informative Hypothesis, Statistics for Social and Behavior Sciences*, ed. P. A. Boelen (Springer, 2008).
30 Allan Drazen, Anna Dreber, Eric Snowberg, et al., "Journal-Based Replication of Experiments," *Journal of Public Economics* 202 (October, 2021): 401–482.

31 Theis Jensen, Bryan Kelly, and Lasse Pedersen, "Is There a Replication Crisis in Finance," *The Journal of Finance* 78, no. 5 (May 26, 2023): 2465–2518; Tim Hasso, Mark Brosnan, Daniel Chai, et al., "Perceived Problems, Causes, and Solutions of Finance Research and Replicability: A Pre-Registered Report," *Pacific-Basin Finance Journal* (October 18, 2024): 1025–1064.
32 J. Scott Armstrong, "Evaluating Forecasting Methods," *Principles of Forecasting: A Handbook for Researchers and Practitioners* (Kluwer Academic Publishers, 2001).
33 G. C. Stephens and M. D. Lazarus, "Twelve Tips for Developing Healthcare Learners' Uncertainty Tolerance," *Medical Teacher* 46, no. 8 (2024): 1035–1043; S. Reis-Dennis, M. S. Gerrity, and G. Geller, "Tolerance for Uncertainty and Professional Development: A Normative Analysis," *Journal of General Internal Medicine* 36, no. 2 (2021): 2408–2413.

What Is an Idea's Cash Value?

Behavioral Science and Pragmatism

Chapter Outline

Introduction

Why are so many of us curious about our own human behavior? The answers to this question overlap with answers to the question opening the previous chapter: What drives us to seek knowledge of the future? Like knowledge of the future, knowledge of human behavior can reduce discomfort with uncertainty and ambiguity. With such knowledge, we feel better equipped to pursue our ambitions and aspirations. We want to ensure that our significant personal and professional choices will result in the life we foresee for ourselves. Indeed, understanding our human nature can be future-oriented: it offers the potential to predict behavior and thus influence others, allowing us to shape events and outcomes.

Fully understanding human behavior, like knowing the future, is a millennia-old quest. Of equal longevity is the effort to leverage insights regarding human behavior to shape our environment. In some times and places, simple forms of magical thinking, such as love potions and incantations, have been trusted methods for influencing outcomes. In other contexts, insights into human motivation and methods of influence have been extremely sophisticated, such as the ancient Greek philosopher Aristotle's writing on persuasion,[1] and the rhetorical techniques developed by the Roman statesman and orator Cicero.[2]

DOI: 10.4324/9781003647034-4

Whilst people may be aware of the insights of ancient philosophers and historical figures, behavioral science is now the go-to source for many of us seeking knowledge of the relationship between human thought, emotion, and action. Definitions of behavioral science vary, yet share common themes. The University of Chicago's Booth School of Business offers a representative definition: "Behavioral science describes the study of human behavior through the use of systematic experimentation and observation," and the synthesis of "theories, concepts, and methodologies across the disciplines of" behavioral economics, cognitive psychology, consumer behavior, social psychology, and sociology.[3] Each of these disciplines employs a version of the scientific method, including formulating hypotheses and gathering data, often in the form of experiments, to prove or disprove hypotheses.

The ascendancy of behavioral science is well documented. For example, according to Washington and Lee University, in recent years the general structure of science has been mapped through analysis of citation data from natural and social sciences journals. Behavioral science, along with mathematics, physics, chemistry, earth sciences, medicine, and the social sciences, has been identified as one of seven major hub sciences. The hub sciences generate research with high rates of citation by scientists across many other fields.[4]

Insights from behavioral science are woven throughout most of our daily lives. If you have tried changing your eating and exercise habits by developing a reward system for yourself, you have been applying concepts from behavioral science. When you seek insights regarding voter or consumer motivations, you are engaging concepts from behavioral science. If you investigate how the family you grew up in affects your own approach to parenting, you are using insights from behavioral science. Moreover, aspects of our daily experience, such as product marketing and public policies related to healthcare and personal finance, are informed by claims of behavioral science.

For many of us, behavioral science's appeal goes beyond its relevance for personal and professional self-improvement and decision making. Behavioral science offers insights regarding the relationships among our evolution, our environment, our thought processes and our actions. In so doing, it seems to answer existential questions most of us ask at some point in our lives. As we develop from adolescents, to young adults, to working professionals, to retirees, most of us wonder periodically "Who am I," "What is the purpose of my life?" and "How much freedom do I really have to make choices about the trajectory of my life." By suggesting evolutionary and environmental explanations for our thought processes and actions, behavioral science offers answers to these questions.[5]

Whilst many people turn to behavioral science to answer both practical and existential questions, they can misinterpret its claims. Through my work facilitating critical thinking seminars in diverse organizations, and serving as a thought partner to executives, I have observed that even highly educated, perceptive professionals can misconstrue behavioral science concepts and recommendations. Like the tendency to be overconfident in forecasts that I have observed among clients, I have found that even astute professionals can be overconfident in behavioral science's ability to predict and influence human behaviors. Such overconfidence has led clients to oversimplify complex situations and propose ineffective, sometimes counterproductive "interventions," hoping to change employee choices, or choices of people in their personal lives. Well-informed professionals can also overinterpret the claims of behavioral science as advocating a deterministic worldview (the idea that all events, including our actions, are determined by causes beyond our control). This deterministic interpretation leads people to underestimate their own capacity to make decisions and create positive change. For example, I have observed clients develop a conception of themselves and others as passive recipients of external influences, losing sight of their own and others' capacity for independent thought and action. Ironically, misunderstanding the findings of behavioral science can lead some people to hasty, poorly informed, ineffective decisions, whilst it can lead others to self-doubt and indecision.

In the course of these various client interactions, I identified several techniques to help them maximize the insights they could gain from behavioral science, without being overconfident in their ability to change other people's behavior, and also without developing a deterministic, ultimately disempowering conception of their own and others' agency. Sharing these techniques with you is this chapter's purpose. I will first share client stories illustrating the types of behavioral science sources many of us consult for guidance. Next, I will highlight how the stories also illustrate common misconceptions regarding the findings of behavioral science. I will then share perspectives and conceptual tools that have helped clients apply what they learn from behavioral science more effectively. These include:

- Considering the limitations of the genre of popular science as a vehicle to understand scientific research accurately.
- Recognizing what defines science and the scientific method.
- Remembering the challenge induction poses for drawing definitive conclusions from certain types of data.
- Understanding critiques of behavioral science methods made by social and natural scientists.

Adopting these perspectives counters the tendency to be overconfident in the findings of behavioral science, particularly as popular sources present them. Employing these perspectives thus counters unrealistic expectations about the success solutions based on behavioral science can have. However, these conceptual practices do no address the second issue mentioned above, the tendency to interpret behavioral science theories deterministically.

In my consultations with clients, I found that they were ultimately able to resolve both issues – overconfidence and overdeterminism – by applying the pragmatic method developed by the American psychologist and philosopher Willam James. James suggests we assess conclusions and theories based on their usefulness – their ability to solve real-world problems – rather than the degree to which they capture objective reality. Due to the iterative nature of scientific research, behavioral science theories, like all scientific theories, evolve. Consequently, no single theory captures the objective reality of human behavior. By shifting attention away from seeking absolute answers to identifying concrete consequences, James's pragmatic method offers a measuring stick for realistically assessing the value of behavioral science findings.

Clients Seeking Guaranteed Outcomes

A long-term client, Marc, engaged me as a thought partner because he faced what he found to be a daunting task. He needed to equip his staff to think more creatively. His organization wanted every department to innovate. Marc was at a loss because his department served a compliance function. His department's purpose of assessing and managing risk seemed at odds with being innovative and creative. Like many of my clients, Marc enjoyed reading and researching on his own. Our sessions often involved discussing his investigations. As I walked toward Marc's office for one of our conversations, I noticed pennants that read "Innovate," dangling from the ceiling. They fluttered playfully as we passed underneath.

When we arrived in his office, he rolled his eyes and said, "If only being creative were as simple as those pennants make it seem." Nonetheless, in our conversation, Marc shared that he had found a solution to his problem – how to equip people habituated to managing risk, keeping things "inside the box," to think creatively. Marc had come across behavioral science research that identified the characteristics of people who are original.[6] I asked Marc to elaborate on the definition of an "original." He explained that originals are people who are non-conformist, are comfortable speaking up and receiving attention, are comfortable with failure, and are motivated by a desire to improve the world. He said further that people who are original have habits that are helpful in a counterintuitive way. For example, people who are original procrastinate in a strategic way. Marc wanted to explore ways to facilitate strategic procrastination, which he believed would help his staff think more creatively. I asked Marc why he found the idea of strategic procrastination compelling enough to implement. He replied that he saw the idea as credible because, in his view, it was proven by scientific experiments that involved surveying and observing the habits of people identified as original thinkers.

Another of my long-term clients, Amanda, starting working with me when she was a mid-level leader at a construction company. Over the course of our work together, Amanda and two colleagues decided to leave the firm and start their own aggregate recycling business. While her colleagues focused on developing their business plan, raising capital, purchasing equipment, and hiring, Amanda focused on business development, attracting businesses to use their services. Amanda, like Marc, was a voracious reader and researcher. In one of our sessions, Amanda relayed insights from some of her recent reading. She was convinced that behavioral science findings about the predictability of people's biased decision making could empower her to create pricing strategies and marketing campaigns. Taking me through her thought process, Amanda explained "We can leverage the typical thinking pitfalls people make to our advantage."[7]

I invited her to elaborate on these pitfalls, and she explained that, for instance, "Research shows that most people care more about avoiding losses than gaining the same amount. When pitching to clients, I should focus on the opportunities they would miss and the money they could lose by *not* using our service." Amanda shared further that she had learned of a technique called "decoy pricing." The decoy, she explained, is an unattractive option that makes the option you want the client to select more attractive. For aggregate removal, she concluded, "We can offer a basic approach, a premium approach, and a third-rate decoy approach that drives people to the premium plan." Amanda said she also learned that people are more likely to stick to commitments they have made in the past. Startups can use this, she explained, by offering prepaid subscriptions or requiring customers to make a commitment before they get a discount. She wondered aloud, "How can I adapt this to our business – should we somehow create memberships?" In response, I asked Amanda to take a step back and share with me why she found the recommendations of her behavioral science source convincing. She responded that the recommendations were based on experiments conducted at institutions such as MIT and Duke University. Considering the findings to be objective and based on observable data, Amanda had confidence in them.

Another thought partner client, Mei, wanted to hone her ability to recognize and hire the best candidates for positions on her team. In one of our conversations, Mei shared with excitement that she had perused several popular behavioral science books, and had discovered research showing that people's quick, first-glance judgments about a situation are often the most accurate. I asked Mei to tell me more, and she stated the concept that really stood out for her was "thin-slicing."[8]

Mei explained that thin-slicing refers to people's ability to make accurate judgments about individuals or situations based on very limited – thin slices – of information, often in a short amount of time. The research showed, according to Mei, that people's best decisions are often based on thin slices. I observed that basing decisions on thin-slicing sounded similar to "going with your gut" to make a decision. Mei agreed, saying that to her, thin-slicing validated relying on her intuitive, instinctive response to a situation to make a decision. She added that she could see advantages to relying on thin-slicing across her organization. "Our sales managers could use thin-slicing to evaluate a salesperson's skills," she mused, "and every manager can use thin-slicing to evaluate employee performance more quickly," she observed.

I asked Mei why the concept of thin-slicing stood out for her. Her answer was partly that it validated her personal experiences and partly that it was based on science. Mei indicated that there were times she ignored her first impression of a candidate and regretted it. "Just because a person went to a great school and has a lot of experience," Mei observed, "does not mean they will be a great fit for your organization or your team." She recalled further, "There have been times when my intuition told me a highly qualified person would still not be a good fit. I didn't listen to that voice, and I wish I had." Mei explained that she found the concept of thin-slicing credible because it encouraged her to trust her intuition, and she could identify experiences where she should have. I asked Mei to say more about the reasons for her confidence that thin-slicing would be an effective approach to the types of personnel decisions she identified. She explained that the author of the book she read sited experiences of experts who could rely on their immediate impressions of people to make very accurate judgments about them, such as one psychologist who could accurately predict the likelihood that a particular couple's relationship would or would not last. "You know," she remarked, "it's based on observable data, science."

A fourth long-term thought partner, Juan, a human resources executive, was frustrated that many employees at his firm did not take advantage of the firm's 401(k) match offered to them. (A 401(k) is an employer-sponsored retirement savings plan, to which employees can make their own contributions.) The firm offered to contribute 6 percent to an employee's 401(k) to match that employee's own 6 percent contribution. Juan was surprised that, despite the incentive of the firm's match, about 20 percent of employees did not make their own 6 percent contribution. In one of our conversations, Juan brightened when he told me he had found the solution to the problem: nudge theory. I asked Juan to tell me about nudge theory, and why he thought nudges would be a more effective way to encourage employee 401(k) contributions than the firm's current approach. Juan explained that nudge theory assumes people do not always make choices that maximize their best interests, which is exactly what he was observing among his firm's employees.[9]

Juan explained further that nudge theory is based on experiments showing that people, when faced with time constraints, or when feeling overwhelmed by the complexity of a particular situation, often use mental shortcuts to make decisions. They rely on rules of thumb, developed through lived experiences, to make decisions quickly (often too quickly). The rules of thumb do not always provide the best guidance for a particular decision. Juan saw this as a realistic account of the way employees make consequential decisions, such as saving for retirement.

I inquired further of Juan how nudge theory addresses people's apparent periodic expediency in decision making. Juan stated that nudges work with the cognitive shortcuts people take. To illustrate, Juan mentioned that a nudge could be based on many people's tendencies to look at the behavior of others as a guide for their own behavior (sometimes called social proof heuristic). Doing what everyone else does – getting on the bandwagon simply because everyone else is on the bandwagon – may not be a helpful mental shortcut, but is can be leveraged in a helpful way, Juan noted. Could people be nudged into contributing their 6 percent to their 401(k)s if they saw (or thought) all their peers were doing it, he asked?

Juan elaborated that another nudge is the default option. A default option is an option that is preselected if an individual does not make an active choice. In fact, Juan explained, he had read that one way to use the default option to nudge people to contribute to their retirement would be for a firm to withhold 6 percent of employees' salaries as their 401(k) contributions. Employees could opt out – they could actively choose not to have the 6 percent contribution withheld. However, Juan asked hypothetically, "How many would opt out? Given their mental shortcuts, wouldn't most employees default to doing the right thing, which is contributing to their retirement?"

As in my conversations with Amanda, Marc, and Mei, I asked Juan why he found the concept of nudging credible. He chuckled and said, "Partly to get on the bandwagon, I guess. A lot of companies and even governments are doing it."[10] We both laughed about his taking a mental shortcut. His real reason, he continued, was the scientific foundation of nudge theory, experiments showing how people exhibit biased thinking and how other people can design circumstances to manipulate that biased thinking.

Although Juan, Mei, Marc, and Amanda consulted different behavioral science sources (psychologists, behavioral economists, and journalists writing popular science), and for different purposes (hiring and developing employees, attracting and retaining customers, implementing human resources policies), I noticed a pattern in their perceptions of their sources. Their excitement and enthusiasm about having found apparently simple, foolproof solutions to their problems reflected misperceptions of their sources' findings. Because their sources used scientific methods, such as testing hypotheses through controlled experiments, my clients viewed their sources' findings as definitive conclusions. In reality, like other sciences, behavioral science develops theories that are subject to revision as new evidence emerges. By seeking guaranteed outcomes, my clients did not recognize that theories, although supported by experiments, are constantly reassessed and refined through the iterative process of research. Applying the theories in day-to-day situations does not guarantee a specific result.

Thus, my clients were overconfident in the success they anticipated when implementing techniques such as decoy pricing, creating default options, deferring to thin-slicing, and facilitating strategic procrastination. Similar to the way other clients, such as Lisa and Elliott, were overconfident in forecasts, Juan, Mei, Marc, and Amanda assumed that implementing strategies based on behavioral science assured them of achieving results, such as dramatic changes in employee and customer choices, immediate success innovating, and a marked surge in the quality of hires.

In essence, Juan, Mei, Marc, and Amanda equated scientific findings generally, and behavioral science finding in particular, with certainty. They consequently assumed that practices and recommendations in popular behavioral science sources would result infallibly in specific behavioral outcomes. To help them use the insights they gained from behavioral science more effectively, I needed to help them contextualize the behavioral science ideas that appealed to them. To do this, I developed several approaches with them, so that they were able to think more realistically about the theories and practices they were discovering in behavioral science and were thus able to develop more effective solutions to their respective problems.

Decrypting Popular Behavioral Science

To say I helped my clients decrypt the popular behavioral science sources they consulted may sound like a contradiction in terms. By definition, if a source is popular, it should not need decrypting. Nonetheless, the genre of popular science generally has limitations that any savvy consumer of information should recognize. Moreover, a high-level understanding of the fundamentals of scientific research is a key tool for accurately interpreting behavioral science sources. Likewise, understanding the similarities and differences between behavioral sciences and natural sciences can enhance your ability to evaluate behavioral science findings. Finally, recognizing that certain assertions, such as those from evolutionary psychology, may currently be more speculative than empirically demonstrated allows you to determine how to apply behavioral science claims in your work and personal life.

Popular science in general, due to its very effort to make scientific information accessible to non-specialists, often oversimplifies complex scientific concepts. Oversimplification, can, in turn, lead to overconfidence in findings, as the foregoing client stories demonstrate. Moreover, popular science sources may draw on extreme, sensational, perhaps unique situations, to attract readers' attention. Rhetorical techniques, such as focusing on the most dramatic aspects of a study, can distort the significance or implications of the research. Most significantly, popular science writers may focus on theories that are already widely accepted and may downplay the iterative nature of scientific inquiry and the uncertainty inherent in it. Like oversimplification, this can give people who are seeking insights and guidance an unwarranted sense of certainty about scientific claims in general, and behavioral science claims in particular.

In addition to recognizing limitations of popular science as a genre, I encouraged my clients to refresh their awareness of scientific methods. Although specific research methods vary across disciplines, the methods of all disciplines share certain components. These include:

- Objective observation and measurement – often, though not always, using mathematics.
- Developing hypotheses – starting points for investigation based on limited existing information.
- Conducting experiments or observing real-life phenomena to test hypotheses.

- Accumulating evidence that a hypothesis captures some aspect of reality.
- Induction: reasoning to establish general rules or conclusions drawn from facts or examples.
- Replication.
- Verification and testing: skepticism regarding results, exposure to scrutiny, peer review, and assessment.[11]

How does this high-level overview of the scientific method address misperceptions of behavioral science claims? It allows you to recognize that science is a process of inquiry, relying on continuous testing and refinement of theories, generating an evolving body of knowledge. This high-level understanding also helps you recognize science is a dynamic process often involving debate, in which different scientists assert competing interpretations of empirical evidence. Recognizing the iterative nature of scientific inquiry, and the often-provisional quality of scientific claims, enables you to maintain realistic expectations regarding the outcomes you anticipate when you put specific behavioral science findings into practice.

The overview of scientific methods suggests another important insight for decrypting the claims of popular behavioral science: bearing in mind the problem of induction. Like all sciences, behavioral science involves induction. The previous chapter introduced a simple way to represent induction: moving from the observation "Some As are Bs" to the conclusion "All As are Bs." Behavioral science uses experiments with select groups of people to generalize about human behavior. For example, the American Psychological Association states that cognitive psychology, which investigates mental processes related to perceiving, thinking, language, and memory relies on inferences from observed behavior.[12] Induction presents the same limitations for behavioral science findings that it does for forecasts. Similar to the use of samples in forecasting, behavioral science involves observing patterns in samples of individual and group behavior, obtained through controlled experiments, then inferring that what is true for the experiment subjects must be true for a parent population (often "all people"). These inferences are the basis for theories about motivation, cognition, social dynamics, and so forth. The inferences involve the assumption that the whole is the same as the sample.

When considering the claims of behavioral science, such as the efficacy of nudging, I encouraged my clients to remember the claims are based on the unproven assumption that the part always represents the whole, that the future always follows past patterns. As with forecasting, behavioral science researchers can compensate for the limitation of induction through replication of experiment results. The more a particular researcher's results are replicated by other researchers, using the same methods, but with different populations, in different times and places, the more likely the conclusions inferred about an entire population are to be accurate for that population. Nonetheless, due to the limitations of induction, and the iterative nature of research, behavioral science claims do not articulate universal laws of human behavior definitively, contrary to what popular sources frequently suggest.

The idea that behavioral sciences can arrive at universal laws in the same way that natural sciences (physics, chemistry, biology, geology, etc.) do is itself debatable. Thus, a fourth perspective I shared with my clients, to help them decrypt behavioral science claims, was the debate among natural and social scientists regarding the most appropriate methods to study people's individual and collective behavior. The scientific methods outlined above originated in the natural sciences, and social scientists generally employ them. However, some thinkers, such as twentieth-century Nobel laureate economist Fredrick Hayek, question the efficacy of applying to human behavior methods originating with natural sciences. Hayek coined the term "scientism," to refer to what he saw as social scientists' excessive trust in the effectiveness of natural science methods applied to all areas of investigation.[13] In the view of Hayek and others, human behavior is too complex to be accurately understood solely through controlled experiments, surveys, statistical hypothesis testing, and induction. For example, people can change their behavior when they know they are being observed, as in experiments, whereas many natural phenomena do not change under observation. (Nonetheless, quantum physicists debate the degree to which observation changes quantum-level activity.) More significantly, specific human behaviors have more causes to isolate than natural phenomena. We are dynamic, we evolve, we have imagination, we can plan, and we have free choice. Because of this, isolating specific variables and drawing definitive, certain conclusions about human actions is illusive.[14]

A fifth perspective I shared with my clients to facilitate their decrypting behavioral science claims was awareness that behavioral scientists disagree regarding which theories can and cannot be empirically demonstrated. For example, some researchers not only seek to explain the workings of mental processes, such as cognitive biases that are the foundation of nudge theory, they also want to establish the origins of mental processes and behaviors.[15] They draw on a related field, evolutionary psychology, to suggest that we have developed thought processes such as biases as survival strategies through our evolution as a species.[16] Such evolutionary claims are often expressed in popular sources by phrases such as, "We are hard-wired to do such and such."

Whilst such theories are plausible, a number of behavioral scientists object that such claims cannot be empirically demonstrated. They observe that there is no way to conduct an experiment to prove or disprove a hypothesis that a certain behavior or thought process results from evolution. In other words, a theory, such as biases developed as survival strategies, is reasonable, yet it is also currently conjecture.[17] I found this fifth perspective was crucial to impart to clients because I observed that such evolutionary claims gave rise to the deterministic perspective described above in the introduction. If we are "hard-wired" to think and do certain things, it sounds like they are inevitable and that we have no control over them. As discussed, clients who developed a deterministic perspective began to underestimate their own capacity to make decisions and create positive change. Helping them recognize that deterministic-sounding assertions are speculative, rather than empirically tested, enabled them to question such assertions, and thus regain a sense of self-efficacy and empowerment.

Assurances Without Absolutes

When I first discussed these guardrails for evaluating recommendations of popular behavioral science sources with Amanda, she exclaimed, "You mean there is nothing I can do to influence my client's decisions and get them to be loyal?" Similarly, upon understanding debates about the application of methods from natural sciences to the study of human behavior, Juan wanted to adopt a hard skepticism about nudging. I assured Amanda and Juan that assessing and employing insights from behavioral science is not a dichotomy between "The claims are true, accept them without question," or "The claims are false, reject them out of hand." Mei was more circumspect, remarking, "I didn't think applying the techniques would be a simple as it sounded." Marc responded optimistically, "I still find the ideas about what makes people original compelling. How can I get them to work for me?"

I realized I needed a way for Juan, Mei, Marc, and Amanda to recognize the value of insights from behavioral science, even without assuming the insights represent infallible, predictable laws of human behavior. I reflected on the way my clients Lisa and Elliott responded when they realized the limitation of induction, and its implication for the reliability of forecasts. Initially, they overcorrected for their former overconfidence in forecasts with a strong skepticism about all forecasts and predictions. I helped them develop a more balanced perspective by exploring with them the role probability calculations play in forecasting. Similarly, I needed a framework to help Juan, Mei, Marc, and Amanda have a balanced perspective regarding their use of behavioral science.

When I considered some clients' deterministic understanding of behavioral science theories, I realized that their use of behavioral science was more complex than clients' use of forecasts. Whilst some clients sought guidance from behavioral science sources to inform business decisions regarding management, marketing, and customer relations, other clients also sought answers to broader existential questions. These included questions about their actual freedom to take actions to change their lives. When thinking about their goals and the trajectories of their lives, clients often wondered about the roles of their genetics, their personal history, and geopolitical circumstances in relation to their autonomy to chart their own paths. Some clients found answers to these classic, nature vs. nurture, free will vs. determinism questions in their exploration of behavioral science. I realized that I needed to offer a framework to guide the application of behavioral science insights to both immediate business decisions and broader existential concerns.

I found the framework in the thinking of the early twentieth century American psychologist and philosopher, William James. Over the course of his career, James developed what he termed the pragmatic method of evaluating ideas, explanations, and theories. I consulted James because he designed his pragmatic method as a way to settle debates about existential issues, such as the existence of free will, which could not be resolved through empirical observation or applying the correspondence theory of truth (discussed in the first chapter of this book). James introduced his pragmatic method in *Principles of Psychology*,[18] where he employed it to evaluate psychological claims about the nature of consciousness, claims that could not be empirically supported through observation. James formally introduced his pragmatic method in *Pragmatism: A New Name for Some Old Ways of Thinking*. He explained that the pragmatic method is designed to settle metaphysical disputes that have proven to be interminable, such as, "Is the world one or many? Fated or free?"[19] He explained further that the pragmatic method starts with the assumption that a particular idea or theory is true and asks what practical difference it will make in anyone's actual life. The pragmatic method asks how the truth will be realized, and what experiences will be different than if the idea or theory were false.[20] James famously summarizes the pragmatic method, explaining that it asks what is the truth's cash value in experiential terms.[21] In other words, for James, the value of a finding or conclusion is not the degree to which it captures an abstraction, such as a transcendent universal principle. Rather, a theory or conclusion's value lies in the improvement it can make in people's lives.

Importantly, James's focus on the practical benefit ideas have on people's lives shifts concern away from pursuing absolute, definitive answers that may not be obtainable. To evaluate an explanation or theory using the pragmatic method, rather than ask "Does a particular conclusion articulate a universal truth?" ask instead "What problem does this conclusion actually solve?" As discussed above, due to the limitation of induction (and other constraints inherent in applying the methods of natural science to the study of human behavior), behavioral science research does not yield definitive conclusions about human behavior. Rather than mistakenly assume it does, or worry that it does not, a pragmatist asks, "What benefit does a particular explanation or theory have for individual's lives?" Pragmatism suggests that if there is a benefit, you should embrace the theory; if there is not a benefit, you can disregard the theory. In other words, from a pragmatist perspective, behavioral science findings have value, not because they purport to articulate universal laws of human behavior, but when there is evidence that they solve practical problems.

Applying the pragmatic method shifted my clients' perception of what they regarded as scientifically derived ideas and practices. Rather than equating science with certainty, thus assuming that behavioral science must produce absolute principles that yield guaranteed behavioral results, my clients reconceived behavioral science claims as useful in a case-by-case, circumstantial, sometimes ad hoc way. As a result of this perceptual shift, Juan, Mei, Marc, and Amanda approached their preferred popular behavioral science sources in a more clinical, detached way. In some sense, they each took on the perspective of a scientist, evaluating the research of other scientists. Juan realized he should create and run an agile experiment to test whether or not the default option nudge would actually prompt more of his firm's employees to invest in their retirement account. He created a timeframe and success metrics and implemented the default option nudge with a small group of employees, rather than all employees. The trial run of the default option nudge indicated that the nudge did not increase the number of employees contributing to their retirement accounts. Most employees in Juan's agile experiment did, in fact, opt out of having a percentage of their salary automatically withheld as their contribution to their 401k. Amanda took a similar approach, creating a pilot program, with a specific timeframe and success metrics. She tested decoy pricing with a sample of new clients and compared the results with those of new clients who did not receive decoy pricing. Amanda had projected that 70 percent of new clients receiving decoy pricing would be nudged into choosing more expensive options. At the end of her designated time frame, she found that only 4 percent of new clients selected more expensive options. Although the result of her experiment did not meet her success metric, Amanda decided to continue using decoy pricing. Implementing it did not require extensive additional effort and the 4 percent increase in clients choosing more expensive options seemed worth the effort.

For Juan and Amanda, the prospect of implementing a behavioral science theory, such as the default option nudge or decoy pricing became an opportunity to run an agile experiment. Marc and Mei applied the pragmatic method more directly to the behavioral science findings that had impressed them. Marc, who had explored the practices that make people original thinkers, asked himself, "What practical difference will it make to my staff's work if we implement strategic procrastination, to promote more creative thinking?" Marc reconsidered his behavioral science source in a more critical way, concluding that the research his source conducted had not been replicated enough to justify implementing the specific practices the source recommended. Using a cost-benefit analysis similar to the one used by Amanda, Marc determined that not enough evidence of the benefit of strategic procrastination existed to be worth the risk of actually encouraging employees to procrastinate.

Similarly, Mei, who had been impressed with the potential of leveraging people's tendency to thin-slice information, asked herself, "What practical different does thin-slicing actually make in the way my colleagues and I perform interviews?" Her answer was that thin-slicing might have significant downsides. Whilst it enables people to work more quickly, she reasoned, it can also lead people to base decisions on their own biases and stereotypes, rather than looking objectively at job applicants and customers. Mei further realized that the expert psychologists her popular behavioral science source presented as illustrations of effective thin-slicing were not a relevant comparison for her and her colleagues. Likewise, the clients who interpreted behavioral science findings deterministically used the pragmatic method to reappraise their own thought processes. They each asked themselves some version of this question: "What practical benefit do I gain from seeing my behaviors as determined by forces beyond my control?" Each client came to a similar conclusion: viewing oneself as subject to determinism does not create a benefit. Rather, it leads to lower self-confidence and decreased effort at self-determination.

After field-testing the perspectives, conceptual tools, and practices outlined in this chapter, clients reported feeling significantly better equipped to leverage insights of behavioral science, particularly as brokered through popular sources. They also reported seeing themselves as even more savvy consumers of information, which in turn increased their sense of competence as problem solvers and decision makers. Their increased sense of competence likewise enhanced their self-confidence in their capacity to pursue the lives they wanted for themselves. Based on these positive client experiences, I offer you the following tools for assessing and applying insights from the behavioral science sources you consult.

Toolkit for Applying Behavioral Science Findings

Tool 1: Manage Expectations for Guaranteed Results

Often, we experience pressure to have an answer for every question, an immediate and unerring solution to every problem. This pressure to guarantee results and outcomes can lead us to have overconfidence in the insights and strategies behavioral science offers. Likewise, popular behavioral science sources may deliberately appeal to our felt need for infallible answers to our questions about our individual and collective behavior. Consequently, managing the need for guaranteed outcomes facilitates your maintaining a realistic perspective regarding the application of insights from popular behavioral science sources to situations in your work and personal life. To manage the need for guaranteed results:

- View problem solving and decision making as a process of discovery in which you acquire new knowledge and capabilities, regardless of the outcomes in a specific situation.
- Avoid perceiving mistakes and missteps as failures. Rather, see them as important experiences that provide you data regarding what insights and techniques work best in different situations. This experiential data equips you to be more prudent in addressing future problems.
- Encourage and inspire yourself by recognizing that the knowledge you gain through the process of discovery strengthens your ability to solve problems and make more effective decisions in the future.

Tool 2: Embrace the Complexity of Human Behavior

The pressure to arrive at definitive answers and solutions often entails a desire to oversimplify complex situations. The more we acknowledge nuances, subtle differences, anomalies, exceptions to the rule, and the like, the more we may be aware that there is not an absolute, "perfect" solution to a problem, or a clearly "right" decision regarding a choice among potential actions. As with the need for guaranteed outcomes, popular behavioral science sources often appeal to people's desire for simplification. In contrast, human behavior is intricate, variable, and evolving. Our behavior involves multiple interconnected factors and cause-effect relationships that are difficult to determine. Like managing the need for guaranteed outcomes, navigating the emotional appeal of oversimplification enhances your ability to apply findings of behavioral science in ways that are efficacious in your real-life circumstances. To embrace more readily the complexity of human behavior:

- Consider what intrigues or fascinates you about people's actions and decisions. Rather than focusing on "people problems" to be solved, focus on what you would like to learn for your own development. Identify questions you have, perhaps about your own needs and motivations, which observing other people can answer.
- View your efforts to analyze and understand complexity as opportunities for you to stay engaged with your work and your personal relationships. Consider intrinsic needs you may have for more interesting, meaningful work, or to make a positive impact on other people's lives. See the task of exploring the intricacies of our behavior as a means to meet some of these intrinsic needs.
- Recognize that acknowledging complexity is the foundation for more reliable solutions. Oversimplification in some sense represents faulty data. When you grapple with complexity you have better accounted for reality. Grounded in your more faithful picture of your reality, your strategies and tactics have a greater likelihood of achieving the results you seek.

Tool 3: Develop a Scientific Mindset

Your mindset involves your perceptions, beliefs, and attitudes toward your lived experiences. Approach the findings of behavioral science, particularly as they are presented in popular sources, using perceptions and perspectives scientists themselves hold. Be mindful that findings of specific experiments and studies are provisional, and likely to be altered, if not disproven, by further research. Be clear that scientific research is an iterative, communal process, even though popular science focuses on a limited number of experiments conducted by well-known researchers. Recognize that when scientists indicate they may have arrived a conclusive finding, perhaps a new universal law, they have participated in a lengthy process of replication, involving many researchers. Developing this scientific mindset equipes you to recognize the value of behavioral science's insights regarding human behavior, without misperceiving them as immutable, definitive statements about human nature.

Tool 4: Be Alert to Disempowering Perspectives

Misperceiving behavioral science findings can lead to perspectives, such as determinism, that are ultimately disempowering. When viewed as articulating immutable laws, claims from behavioral science may lead to the assumption that our actions and choices are determined by some source beyond ourselves, perhaps genetics, evolution, or both. By the same token, overestimating the predictive power of behavioral science claims may lead to the assumption that we can successfully manipulate others for our purposes when we apply certain psychological tools. Both of these assumptions are ultimately disempowering.

Seeing ourselves as simply acted upon by forces beyond our control undermines our ability to meet intrinsic needs, such as the sense that we are competent in various aspects of our lives and that we have autonomy. The assumption of determinism likewise inhibits our ability to gain self-confidence by seeing ourselves actively determining our own courses of action. In a similar way, if we see ourselves as possessing verified methods to influence other people's choices and actions to align with our plans, we can also disempower ourselves by investing time and effort in practices than cannot give us the results we expect. Moreover, we can engage in actions that infringe on other people's autonomy, damaging our relationships with them.

Awareness of the potential for these assumptions is itself the conceptual tool. To get the most value from behavioral science sources, avoid these deterministic assumptions. Remember that these assumptions are not inherent in behavioral science and embracing insights from behavioral science does not require you accept determinism.

Tool 5: Practice Conceptual Agility

Conceptual agility is the capacity to adapt to new ideas and situations. It helps you assimilate new information quickly, leverage what you already know, and embrace change. The relationship between conceptual agility and the pragmatist theory of knowledge discussed in this chapter is symbiotic. Adopting the pragmatist point of view regarding the value of behavioral science findings can facilitate your conceptual agility, whilst adopting pragmatism itself involves such agility.

As just discussed, pragmatism assesses ideas in terms of their usefulness to solve immediate problems, rather than their ability articulate absolute, transcendent claims about aspects of reality. Pragmatism thus entails an ongoing process of evaluation and revision. It involves rejecting ideas that no longer help you solve problems and scanning for new ideas that will help you. This ongoing process requires conceptual agility. To facilitate your use of the pragmatic theory of knowledge:

- Deliberately seek out new experiences. This allows you to scan for new ideas continually and replace ideas that are no longer useful. Moreover, it keeps you mentally nimble. New experiences do not need to be dramatic adventures. For example, just exploring a part of your home area you have never visited before requires you to figure out new street arrangements, look for landmarks, practice your observation skills, and engage your ability to analyze and synthesize new information.

- Remember that one of the most effective means to prepare for significant unexpected, unpredicted events is routinely to seek out low-risk, micro-experiences of things you find unfamiliar. Like practicing a sport or musical instrument, these micro-experiences prepare you for the actual performance of life.

Progress Journal

You can sustain changes in your thinking in a similar way to the way you might change habits, such as what you eat and how much you exercise. Track your progress by keeping a journal of how you implement new ideas, noting which are easy to apply and where you run into challenges.

Progress Journal – Week 1

Weekly Self-Reflection

- What claims or findings based on scientific methods did you encounter this week (work situations, personal situations, other)?
- Which tools did you apply to those findings (for example, a scientific mindset, conceptual agility, pragmatism)?
- What questions did you ask to contextualize and better understand the scientific sources you consulted?
- What insights did you gain about the situation the scientific sources were intended to inform?

Pulse-Check

0	1	2	3	4	5	6	7	8	9	10
Not at all			Somewhat					Absolutely		

Using the scale given above, rate your degree of confidence below by recording a number from 0 to 10 in the column on the right.

Please rate how confident you are that you can:

Apply awareness of scientific methods to a scientific source's claims	
Appraise behavioral science findings using the pragmatic method	
Identify potentially disempowering perspectives	
Manage expectations for guaranteed results	
Practice conceptual agility	

Progress Journal – Week 2

Weekly Self-Reflection

- What claims or findings based on scientific methods did you encounter this week (work situations, personal situations, other)?
- Which tools did you apply to those findings (for example, a scientific mindset, conceptual agility, pragmatism)?
- What questions did you ask to contextualize and better understand the scientific sources you consulted?
- What insights did you gain about the situation the scientific sources were intended to inform?

Pulse-Check

0	1	2	3	4	5	6	7	8	9	10
Not at all			Somewhat						Absolutely	

Using the scale given above, rate your degree of confidence below by recording a number from 0 to 10 in the column on the right.

Please rate how confident you are that you can:

Apply awareness of scientific methods to a scientific source's claims	
Appraise behavioral science findings using the pragmatic method	
Identify potentially disempowering perspectives	
Manage expectations for guaranteed results	
Practice conceptual agility	

Progress Journal – Week 3

Weekly Self-Reflection

- What claims or findings based on scientific methods did you encounter this week (work situations, personal situations, other)?
- Which tools did you apply to those findings (for example, a scientific mindset, conceptual agility, pragmatism)?
- What questions did you ask to contextualize and better understand the scientific sources you consulted?
- What insights did you gain about the situation the scientific sources were intended to inform?

Pulse-Check

0	1	2	3	4	5	6	7	8	9	10
Not at all					Somewhat					Absolutely

Using the scale given above, rate your degree of confidence below by recording a number from 0 to 10 in the column on the right.

Please rate how confident you are that you can:

Apply awareness of scientific methods to a scientific source's claims	
Appraise behavioral science findings using the pragmatic method	
Identify potentially disempowering perspectives	
Manage expectations for guaranteed results	
Practice conceptual agility	

Progress Journal – Week 4

Final Self-Reflection and Assessment

- How has your approach to appraising behavioral science sources and findings changed in the past four weeks?
- How has your perception of findings based on scientific methods changed in the past four weeks?
- What are two to three situations in which you feel you used the pragmatic method effectively to solve a problem or make a decision?
- Describe a situation in which you could have used the pragmatic method more effectively. What would you do differently?
- What skills or habits of mind do you need to enhance going forward?
- What resources and support do you need to continue to develop skills?

Notes

1 Aristotle, *Rhetoric*, eds. Edward Meredith Cope and John Edwin Sandys (Cambridge University Press, 2010).
2 Cicero, *On Oratory and Orators,* ed. and trans. J. S. Watson (Southern Illinois University Press, 1986).
3 From the website of the University of Chicago Booth School of Business's Mindworks Institute, https://www.chicagobooth.edu/mindworks/what-is-beh avioral-science-research. In some instances, people use the term behavioral science to refer specifically to research regarding cognitive biases and its application to public policy and marketing through nudge theory. Nudge theory is the idea that an organization can present a population with choices designed to engage their cognitive biases, leveraging these biases so that the population makes choices the organization deems as desirable and in that population's best interest. I will use a broader view of what qualifies as behavioral science, reflecting the fact that my clients consult multiple sources that self-identify as behavioral science sources, including organizational psychologists, cognitive psychologists, social psychologists, behavioral economists, and journalists writing popular science.
4 Website of Washington and Lee University Department of Cognitive and Behavioral Science (formerly the Department of Psychology), https://www.wlu. edu/academics/areas-of-study/cognitive-and-behavioral-science.
5 For a description of the ecological and evolutionary theories in psychology, see Johan E. Korteling, Anne-Marie Brouwer, and Alexander Toet, "A Neural Network Framework for Cognitive Bias," *Frontiers in Psychology* 9 (September 2, 2018), https://www.frontiersin.org/journals/psychology/articles/ 10.3389/fpsyg.2018.01561/full.
6 Marc was interpreting ideas he gained from reading Adam Grant, *Originals: How Non-Conformists Move the World* (Penguin, 2017).
7 Amanda was interpreting ideas she gained from reading Dan Ariely, *The Upside of Irrationality: The Unexpected Benefits of Defying Logic* (Harper-Collins, 2011).
8 Mei was interpreting ideas she gained from Malcolm Gladwell, *Blink: The Power of Thinking Without Thinking* (Little, Brown, 2005).
9 Eric was interpreting ideas he had gained from reading sources such as Cass R. Sunstein and Richard H. Thaler, *Nudge: Improving Decisions About Health, Wealth and Happiness* (Penguin, 2008), as well as articles such as Richard B. Chase and Sriram Dasu, "Want to Perfect Your Company's Service? Use Behavioral Science," *Harvard Business Review*, June 2001. Eric also consulted sources such as Harvard University's "Nudge U" blog, www.nudgeu. harvard.edu.
10 There is an increasing body of literature that questions the efficacy of nudging as currently practiced by business and government. See, for example, Jens Koed Madsen, Lee de Wit, Peter Ayton, et al., "Behavioral Science Should Start by Assuming People Are Reasonable," *Trends in Cognitive Science* 28, no. 7 (July, 2024): 583–585. Likewise, see Christopher J. Bryan, Elizabeth Tipton, and David S. Yeager, "Behavioural Science Is Unlikely to Change the World Without a Heterogeneity Revolution," *Nature Human Behavior*, August 5, no. 8 (2021): 981–989. Also see Evan Polman and Sam J. Maglio, "Will Your Nudge Have a Lasting Impact," *Harvard Business Review*, April 29, 2024.
11 This list is adapted from the definition of science offered by the Science Council, https://sciencecouncil.org/about-science/our-definition-of-science/.

The Science Council is an organization in the United Kingdom, established by Royal Charter in 2003, and a Competent Authority with respect to the European Union directive 2005/36/EC. Its members represent 350,000 scientists. The definition offered by the Science Council reflects a number of definitions offered by scientific member organizations.

12 American Psychological Association, "Cognitive Psychology," *Dictionary of Psychology*, www.dictonary.apa.org/cognitive-psychology.

13 The original lecture was given in 1974; it was later reprinted in 1989, see F. A. Hayek, "The Pretense of Knowledge," *The American Economic Review* 79, no. 6 (December, 1989): 3–7.

14 Drew H. Bailey, Alexander J. Jung, Adriene M. Beltz, et al., "Causal Inference on Human Behavior," *Nature Human Behavior* 8, no. 8 (August, 2024): 1448–1459.

15 Other examples include Michael Shermer's evolutionary explanation of superstitious beliefs. See Michael Shermer, *The Believing Brain: From Ghosts and Gods to Politics and Conspiracies – How We Construct Beliefs and Reinforce Them as Truths* (Macmillan, 2011). Likewise, Jonathan Haidt offers evolutionary explanations of the origins of moral foundations. See Jonathan Haidt, *The Righteous Mind: Why Good People are Divided by Politics and Religion* (Penguin Random House, 2013).

16 Johan E. Korteling, Anne-Marie Brouwer, and Alexander Toet, "A Neural Network Framework for Cognitive Bias," *Frontiers in Psychology* 9 (September 2, 2018), https://www.frontiersin.org/journals/psychology/articles/10.3389/fpsyg.2018.01561/full.

17 Some philosophers and psychologists propose that behavioral science, when making assertion regarding, e.g., free will, determinism, personal identity, and the existence of a mind independent of the physical brain, actually shifts into the traditionally philosophical activity of metaphysics. For example, theories in behavioral economics and social psychology describe how social factors influence behavior, suggesting a metaphysical account of human behavior that is consistent with empirical data. Likewise, some philosophers and psychologists are exploring ways insights from philosophical metaphysics enhances behavioral science, for example by helping behavioral scientists clarify what they mean by fundamental terms such as behavior, cause, and mental process. See, for example, Greg Henriques, "The Metaphysical Mysteries of Life, Mind and Culture," *Psychology Today*, May 29, 2020; and Julian C. Leslie, "The Relevance of Metaphysics for Behavior Analysis," *Perspectives on Behavior Science* 44 (March, 2021): 29–40. For a groundbreaking discussion of metaphysics based on empirical observation rather than abstract, logical speculation, see Peter Strawson, *Individuals: An Essay in Descriptive Metaphysics* (Routledge, 1964).

18 William James, "The Mind-Stuff Theory," *Principles of Psychology*, Volumes 1–2 (Harvard University Press, 1983), Chapter VI.

19 William James, "Lecture II: What Pragmatism Means," *Pragmatism: A New Name for Some Old Ways of Thinking* (Meyers Education Press, 2019), 45.

20 William James, "Lecture II: What Pragmatism Means," *Pragmatism: A New Name for Some Old Ways of Thinking* (Meyers Education Press, 2019), 45.

21 William James, "Lecture II: What Pragmatism Means," *Pragmatism: A New Name for Some Old Ways of Thinking* (Meyers Education Press, 2019), 45.

Chapter 5

How Do I Know I'm Doing the Right Thing?

Trusting Your Own Judgment

Chapter Outline

Introduction

When have you been in a situation in which no amount of expert advice or counsel delineated a particular course of action as being clearly right for you? Perhaps at one time you wondered how you would tell your parents you wanted to pursue a different career from the one they anticipated for you. A friend likely shared with you how they had the same conversation, but you finally had to create your own approach. Perhaps at a certain point you had to choose between a role that would advance a public good or a role that would be lucrative. You might have appraised your options using one of a number of decision analysis techniques. You might have asked a family member how they navigated a similar situation. In the end, you had to align your choice with your own values and self-perception. Perhaps you faced a challenge that you were not motivated to surmount and hoped for a way to save face with friends and family. Rather than say "I'm really not interested in overcoming this thing, I just want to go in a different direction," you may anonymously have asked for guidance from an advice columnist. Still, you had to identify for yourself what you

DOI: 10.4324/9781003647034-5

wanted from your own life, and to determine if sidestepping the challenge would ultimately allow you to go where you wanted to go in the long term.

For personal situations such as these, many of us *seek* expert advice. In some instances, such personal choices are actually precipitated by receiving expert advice (such as medical diagnoses or legal counsel). Likewise, in these personal situations, most of us seek insights from friends, family, and perhaps advice columns or even ethics columns. Ultimately, in these situations, we nonetheless have to rely on our own personal judgment. No source we seek out for guidance has our exact life experience. They do not see us as we see ourselves. They do not know the fears and aspirations only each of us knows about ourselves. In this chapter, I will share how I have helped clients enhance their personal judgment in order to navigate such personal situations with greater clarity and self-awareness.

This chapter thus differs somewhat from the previous three. In the previous chapters, we reviewed three categories of expert sources people commonly turn to for guidance in different aspects of their lives: public discourse; forecasts and predictions; and popular behavioral science. Each chapter has offered tools to examine critically sources that are equally expert but have competing points of view, or that offer purportedly simple, certain solutions, and seemingly incontrovertible data for decision making. This chapter offers an approach to situations in which you immediately see that a quick, simple, certain solution does not exist, and you recognize that the answer you seek is beyond the scope of any expert advice to provide. Nonetheless, the conceptual tools offered in the previous three chapters contribute to your refining your personal judgment. This chapter allows you to build on the insights you gained in the previous three, now more deliberately focusing on self-awareness to enhance your personal judgment.

To understand the type of personal situations we will address in this chapter, let us reflect on a specific situation. Consider an elementary school girl who has kidney disease and is struggling, even on dialysis. Her physicians are considering a kidney transplant, although it is not clear the transplant will be successful. The girl's siblings are too young to be donors and her mother is not histocompatible. However, her father is compatible.

When learning of his compatibility with his daughter, the father is unsure what to do. There is a slight possibility of a cadaver kidney becoming available. Even so, the medical staff say his daughter's prognosis after the transplant is very uncertain. The father is also concerned about the amount of suffering his daughter has already experienced. Moreover, the father is concerned about his ability to provide for his other two children, should he choose to give a kidney to his daughter. Although this particular example involves a biomedical situation (in fact it is a case I used when I taught biomedical ethics[1]), it more generally illustrates a personal dilemma.

In my experience, people often assume a dilemma is explicitly ethical, involving the choice between what many of us would describe as the lesser of two evils. The "trolley-car problem" thought experiment illustrates this type of dilemma. In the thought experiment, a trolley-car is running out of control toward five people tied to the trolley-car track. A bystander has the option to divert the trolley-car to a sidetrack where only one person is tied to the track. This scenario poses an ethical dilemma: should you willingly kill one person to save the lives of five other people. While the trolley-car problem can be a useful teaching tool, helping people explore and practice their capacity for ethical reasoning, it is not as subtle as our real-life dilemmas. The case of the father who medically qualifies to donate a kidney to his daughter, but nonetheless has reservations about doing so, more realistically illustrates the kinds of real-life personal dilemmas I have experienced with my clients.

What does the case of the father's potential kidney donation have in common with other personal dilemmas? His case first illustrates that personal dilemmas usually do not involve explicitly ethical decisions between "two evils," such as the decision to kill one person to save five, or to allow five to die to avoid willfully harming one. In the father's case, there are not two obvious "evils." There are, rather, facts, needs, and interests that appear to compete with one another. The father's case involves more subtle questions about fair distribution of resources, loyalty, fidelity, and addressing tensions among duties to other people. Second, the case illustrates that dilemmas cannot be resolved simply by appeals to expert advice, because they involve values as much as facts. The expert medical opinion that the success the of the daughter's transplant is uncertain cannot tell the father if the chance would be worth it for his daughter. This is a question of values, such as the value of extending life and the value of quality of life.

The case also illustrates that a defining feature of dilemmas is that they elicit from us deliberation, rather than obvious application of specific guidance, rules, and recommendations. We are aware we face a dilemma when we immediately have to pause and ask ourselves, "What *is* the right thing to do here?" To answer this, we often struggle to assess our beliefs, while using our imaginations to rehearse various courses of action.[2] Although personal dilemmas may not be an obvious choice between "two evils," I have found they often involve competing positive goals, such as financial success and helping other people, or providing access to a limited set of resources, for instance distributing resources to employees or family members.

Through four stories of clients facing personal dilemmas, this chapter will introduce you to a method of refining your personal judgment, so that you can better address your own personal dilemmas, feel more confident as a decision maker, and ultimately feel more satisfied with your decisions. The method to refine personal judgment outlined in this chapter, which I developed working with clients, involves building your capacity for ethical reasoning by understanding and applying six types of ethical perspectives, relevant to all dilemmas. Although you can read this chapter by itself, it is designed to serve as a capstone for this book. Thus, there are more application activities than in the previous chapters. The application activities invite you to self-assess your reasoning preferences and give you an opportunity to refine your personal judgment by examining a series of dilemmas using the six types of ethical theory described in the chapter.

Clients Facing Dilemmas

As we begin to explore the contours of personal dilemmas, it is important to distinguish dilemmas from what might be called advice-column questions. To be sure, clients and seminar participants have asked me advice-column questions. These questions are tactical, such as "How should I talk to a neurodiverse colleague," and "Should I tell colleagues in advance I'm marrying a co-worker?" When someone asks questions like these, they want a specific recommendation about what to do or how to act in a particular situation.[3] In some sense, they want options that they can try on for size. When I offer specific guidance in response to an advice-column question, I do not assume the receiver is going to do exactly what I recommend. I anticipate that they will do what feels right to them, but that they want to understand a range of possible courses of action, each of which could work in their particular situation. I can answer such questions by suggesting tips, or offering a quick burden-benefit analysis of different courses of action. Advice-column questions are important, and they usually reflect a pressing concern on the part of the person asking the question. Yet, the topics of advice-column questions are not characterized by the tensions between goals, values, and obligations that define dilemmas. At the same time, if you peruse popular advice columns, you will find that people often submit questions about dilemmas. The binary question-and-answer format of advice columns cannot adequately facilitate the deliberation that these dilemmas require. While an astute advice columnist can offer insightful self-reflection questions, advice columns are not, as a genre, dynamic enough to help you discern how to move forward at a critical juncture that is characterized by competing claims and obligations.

The client stories I share below illustrate such critical junctures, which require more than advice to navigate. The client stories I have narrated in previous chapters, describing client responses to forecasts and behavioral science findings, have illustrated that people are often overconfident in expert advice, particularly recommendations derived from statistics and the scientific method. Clients believe that implementing such advice will lead to guaranteed results. In contrast, when facing dilemmas, clients are not overconfident. Rather they recognize they have hit a limit of expert advice – statistics and science can provide information, but they cannot themselves tell you which course of action is best for you. In other words, the client stories I recounted in Chapters 3 and 4 illustrate overconfidence in the face of uncertainty. The client stories in this chapter illustrate a range of emotions, from confusion to frustration to angst in the face of uncertainty. Clients' responses to uncertainty in these cases are different from the previous situations because dilemmas are, inherently, patently uncertain. Dilemmas, by their nature, do not present the opportunity to be overconfident. When facing a dilemma, you may immediately feel puzzled, stumped, even stuck, with no clear path forward. I hope the following client stories resonate with your experiences. The stories illustrate common types of personal dilemmas I have helped clients navigate.

The first story I would like to share involves Simon, whom I met when giving a talk at an international biomedical research and public health organization. My talk was about decision making. Simon approached me afterward indicating he faced a big decision and he would like my counsel. I had the rest of the afternoon free, so we walked to a coffee shop adjacent to the institute's campus. Simon was a cancer researcher in his mid-30s, having impressively earned an MD and a PhD in biology. He had come to the institute on a three-year postdoctoral research fellowship. He was approaching the end of his third year, and had been offered a permanent research position at the institute.

Simon explained the offer was in many respects his dream job. He had studied medicine because his mother had died of cancer when he was a child. That experience, and his mathematical acumen, oriented him to a career in public health. He was motivated by a desire to address global health issues and to reduce health disparities. Plus, Simon explained, he genuinely enjoyed research and spending hours in a lab. "Where is the decision?" I asked, "It sounds like there is nothing to think about. Just say yes." Simon replied, "Well, my spouse would like me to maximize my profit potential. I could make about 35 percent more at a pharmaceutical company than I will make here. Over the course of my career, that adds up to several million dollars." I observed, "You would still be helping people if you worked in private industry. If you made more, as well, what is the source of your hesitation?" Simon replied, "I'm not really sure I would be helping people in the private sector. I might spend my career working on a compound that treats a condition only affecting a small population, but a population that can afford prescriptions." I tried to paraphrase, "So, you would miss the *public* in public health?" Simon responded "Exactly, the main reason I entered this field, besides enjoying the work and being good at it, was to work on curing a disease that affects a lot of people." Simon indeed faced a dilemma, a choice between competing goals and obligations. His own goals, his spouse's needs and expectations, the possibility of making a significant difference in other people's lives, and the possibility of a materially comfortable future were all in tension.

Similarly, another client, Aviva, consulted me when she faced a situation of competing goals. Aviva was the executive director of a non-profit civic service membership organization. The organization was involved in a number of projects, among them partnering with the United States Department of State to resettle in the United States refugees from a country experiencing a civil war. One club member had become extremely involved in the refugee resettlement effort. A business person, the club member was an extremely good fundraiser. By organizing a series of special events, the club member had raised a sum of six figures in emergency assistance for the refugees, as well as thousands more dollars of in-kind donations, primarily vehicles for the refugees to use as transportation to their jobs and English as a Second Language (ESL) classes.

Aviva explained to me that the organization's volunteer treasurer had come to her, overwhelmed and worried. Aviva shared with me, "The treasurer said she did not sign up to handle this level of transactions, in addition to handling our club's routine business. She's starting to feel taken advantage of, even though she knows all the extra fundraising and donations are for an important cause." Aviva explained further, "The treasurer is also worried that our particular type of non-profit designation doesn't allow us to accept the volume of donated vehicles now coming in. So, our non-profit status could be in jeopardy if we continue down this path." Aviva continued, "I've spoken with the member about the issues the treasurer raised, and they said they might leave the club if we don't continue to support the refugee resettlement initiative at the current level. The member is convinced the refugee resettlement is the only truly impactful project we have." Aviva concluded, "I can't believe I'm in this predicament – I took this role because I wanted to be part of a systemic social change, not just a Band-Aid or feel-good program. And now I feel like I have to basically fire a member, whom I actually support, in order to fulfill my fiduciary responsibilities as executive director." Like Simon, Aviva faced a dilemma, although of a slightly different sort. Where Simon encountered tensions between his desire to do good, his desire to have a strong relationship with his spouse, and his desire for a comfortable living, Aviva encountered tensions between her role as an executive, the need to protect an organization benefiting a number of people, her relationship with an individual member, and her own motivation to make systemic changes in social problems.

A third client, Varsha, an HR executive, was responsible for deciding which of her firm's employees would receive tuition assistance to pursue MBAs. Varsha worked for a mid-sized financial organization, and her budget typically allowed her to pay full tuition for five MBAs per year. Employees seeking an MBA usually followed an executive MBA at a nearby state university. Varsha scheduled a conversation with me, indicating she faced a conundrum. When we met, she explained that a very talented employee had been accepted to an Ivy League MBA program. The company saw a great deal of potential in the employee and could anticipate that equipping her with an MBA would quickly be a financial benefit to the firm. Ideally, it would also induce the employee to build a career with the firm. "The problem is," Varsha explained, "the tuition for the Ivy League program is as much as three MBAs at our local state university. If I agree to pay for her degree, there are three people I won't be able to fund this year."

The situation seemed to lend itself to a burden-benefit analysis. I suggested this, and Varsha replied, "I tried that and it didn't get me anywhere. I see equal burdens and benefits for each option." She continued, "Candidly, the employees accepted to the local executive MBA program this year are not stars. They would not get into a more prestigious program. But, they are loyal, highly competent, hardworking, long-term employees, and I feel they deserve for us to pay for their degree." She stated further, "For this younger employee to pursue the Ivy League degree would make such a huge difference for her. Really, she would not be going from good to great, but from great to even greater. She would be much more valuable to the company with a strong MBA than the other three will be with local executive MBAs." Varsha concluded that she faced a dilemma, which she felt challenged to resolve using the decision-making methods she had used in other situations. Varsha's dilemma had some features similar to Aviva's. The crux involved fairly distributing a resource (tuition assistance) in a way that would most benefit her organization. Like Aviva, Varsha was also concerned about maintaining long-term relationships and recognizing the important work of specific individuals.

A fourth long-term client, Matt, was very accomplished, holding a BA in engineering from an elite school and a JD. His dual degree positioned him uniquely to work as a general counsel for a global construction company. While we worked together, the firm offered him the position of chief operating officer for North America. Prior to the promotion offer, his spouse passed away, leaving him the sole parent of his two adolescent children. Also prior to the promotion offer, Matt's widowed father developed Alzheimer's disease. An only child, Matt had moved his father into his home. Matt was a successful executive, primary parent to two adolescent children, and primary caregiver to a parent with dementia, all at the same time.

When Matt called to tell me about the promotion, I immediately invited him to dinner to celebrate. He replied, "I appreciate the invitation, but I'm not sure I'm in the mood to celebrate. I really feel conflicted about this offer." I asked him to elaborate. He sighed, saying "There is no way I can keep doing everything at once. A promotion like this has always been my dream. But I never thought when it came, if I came, the rest of my life would be so crazy."

I encouraged Matthew to say more. He continued, "I never saw myself being a single parent and caregiver. This new promotion would require me to travel most of the year. I couldn't reasonably have any caretaking roles." I asked what solutions he was already considering. "Trust me," he said, "this new role comes with a seven-figure salary. I can easily send both kids to boarding school – they are both old enough – and put my father in a first-rate facility." "But ...?" I began. "But," Matt continued, "I'm not sure I want to institutionalize my father, at least not yet. He still has some good days where he recognizes me. And, I don't want to miss out on the next few years with my children. They'll be off to college and on their own in five years, tops." Matt concluded, "I never thought I'd feel this way about such good news, but I just feel caught in a bind. Why couldn't this offer have come at a different time, or why couldn't my personal life be what I expected?"

Matt's dilemma is perhaps most like Simon's. At stake are competing professional and personal claims, as well as competing ambitions and motivations, such as the desire to advance professionally, to enjoy prestige and affluence, and enjoy irreplaceable time with family members. Each of these client stories illustrates that a defining feature of dilemmas is that they cannot be resolved by "applying" data and methods. Addressing dilemmas requires deliberation, which is a dynamic process. Because they involve your own values, motivations, and aspirations, dilemmas are most effectively addressed by having a refined sense of your own personal judgment. While exercising personal judgment involves accurately assessing credible information (which the conceptual tools in the previous chapters will help you do), it also involves consideration of personal beliefs and values. Refining your personal judgment thus involves both applying concepts, such as the limitations of induction, the correspondence theory of truth, and self-awareness about the ways your values inform your decisions. The remainder of this chapter focuses on the last of these. Based on the experience of helping clients navigate personal dilemmas by refining their personal judgment, I offer you the tools in the remainder of this chapter. I hope they will equip you, as they have others, to approach personal dilemmas in ways that bring greater clarity and satisfaction with the choices you make.

Refining Your Personal Judgment

One way to refine personal judgment in relation to dilemmas is to categorize the dilemmas themselves. As discussed, the word dilemma often connotes specifically ethical dilemmas. Simon, Aviva, Varsha, and Matt's stories nonetheless illustrate that personal dilemmas are often not explicitly ethical. Whether explicitly ethical or not, dilemmas always involve tensions between competing elements: competing relationships, competing obligations, competing goals and aspirations, and competing interests. Various thinkers have proposed different typologies for dilemmas. For example, the journalist Rushworth Kidder suggests that dilemmas are of four essential types: truth vs. loyalty; individual vs. community; short-term gain vs. long-term gain; and justice vs. mercy.[4] An alternative typology classes dilemmas as individual-level; organizational-level; structural-level.[5]

These typologies are helpful up to a point. For example, Aviva's dilemma might be categorized as an organizational-level dilemma, while Varsha's dilemma might be both an organizational-level dilemma and an individual vs. community dilemma. In contrast, Simon and Matt's dilemmas do not fit neatly into Kidder's categories. Their dilemmas might be categorized as individual rather than organizational, but such categorization does not provide insight about a resolution to the dilemmas. Thus, while I have shared with my clients such categories, I have observed that categorizing is not sufficient for them to navigate their dilemmas. Effective personal judgment involves additional components.

When I first described for Aviva the practice of refining her personal judgment, she responded saying that she had always heard, "When in doubt, go with your gut." She had also been reading an influential social psychologist. "His research shows," Aviva explained, "that our moral judgments about situations are mainly intuitive."[6] Aviva elaborated, "Apparently, we have intuitions that are part of our evolution. We see situations in pairs, such as fairness or cheating and care or harm."[7]

Based on her reading, Aviva questioned the idea of developing personal judgment. "It seems like," she commented, "we have automatic responses to situations." I asked if this was true for Aviva and the dilemma she faced regarding her fiduciary responsibility to her organization and her commit-ment to the refugee resettlement initiative. She replied, "I honestly don't have an intuition. My gut isn't telling me anything. I feel like I'm experi-encing a solar flare interrupting a satellite transmission." "So, in your cur-rent situation," I suggested, "you do not have an automatic response? Does your situation involve something like care vs. harm or fairness vs cheating?" She thought for a moment and answered, "I *don't* have an automatic response. The situation could be fairness vs cheating, but not really. No party is trying to cheat. They have different ideas of what the right thing to do is." Aviva paused, then went on, "If I try to apply the framework I have been reading about, I would say both parties in my dilemma want to be fair, they just have different ideas about what fairness looks like. But, I'm not sure 'fair' is really the right term."

I clarified for Aviva that part of what defines a dilemma is often *not* having an immediate intuitive or gut response. If you are encountering a situation that is new for you, and do not have similar previous experiences to draw on, you may not have an internal source for an intuitive response. "So," she observed, "I guess that is why developing my personal judg-ment is important – for times when my 'gut' kind of fails me." I appreci-ated Aviva's response. Until I invited her to reflect on her experience, she assumed dilemmas were best resolved by reliance on instinctive responses. Only when she realized that her dilemma actually stymied her intuitive response did the relevance of personal judgment for addressing dilemmas become clear for her.

Where Aviva first responded to the idea of refining personal judgment by asking about the role of intuition, Matt compared personal judgment to conscience. I invited Matt to elaborate on his understanding of conscience. He shared, "I guess it's like an inner voice. It tells me if something seems right or wrong, not just if it's practical or easy." With Aviva's comment in mind, I queried, "Do you experience your conscience as an immediate, say, intuitive response to a situation?" Matt replied, "No. I would say it's often in contrast to a gut response. What I think is right can be different from my first response to a situation." He continued, "My conscience is more like a voice saying, 'Hey, wait a minute before you do that.'"

After hearing Matt's self-assessment, I agreed that personal judgment regarding dilemmas involves what many people refer to as their conscience. As self-reflection undertaken to determine what is right in a given situ-ation, conscience involves analysis of your potential actions: Is an action right or wrong; obligatory or optional; good or bad? In other words, conscience involves your awareness of and reflection on your potential actions in relation to your own standards. Matt was not the only client to reference conscience when I introduced the idea of refining personal judgment as an approach to dilemmas. Their observations gave me an insight. Personal judgment involves a range of cognitive activities, which include not only weighing information and drawing conclusions, but also the ability to evaluate the ethical aspects of a situation.

While many personal dilemmas often are not explicitly ethical (in the sense of the trolley-car thought experiment), the capacity for informed ethical analysis is crucial for approaching dilemmas because they inherently involve tensions between ethical considerations, such as obligations, duties, balancing individual and collective interests, and the like. Reflecting on this insight in relation to my academic background, I realized that a key means to help my clients enhance their personal judgment was to share with them a range of philosophical ethical theories (which in some ways overlap with the theories of truth discussed in Chapter 2). Matt, Aviva, Varsha, Simon, and other clients have found that understanding ethical theory enhanced their ability to analyze and resolve personal dilemmas. This awareness has provided them with different perspectives and principles to consider when deliberating about the conflicting concerns and obligations that compose personal dilemmas.

Ethical Reasoning and Personal Judgment

Over the course of multiple conversations, I ultimately shared with my clients six specific types of ethical theories developed by philosophers. The six types of ethical theory are:

- Consequentialism
- Utilitarianism
- Deontology
- Rights-based
- Communitarian
- Care-based

I curated the theories based on what I thought my clients would find most useful, helping them with their deliberations and using a bit of trial and error. After outlining the theories for you, I will return to the dilemmas involving Simon, Aviva, Varsha, and Matt, sharing which theories they found most useful and how they resolved their dilemmas. With each client, I started with an ethical theory called consequentialism. I started with consequentialism because people are often already familiar with a specific form of consequentialism, utilitarianism. According to utilitarianism, the best action is that which produces the greatest good for the greatest number of people.[8] More generally, consequentialism assesses actions according to the balance of their good or bad consequences. From a consequentialist perspective, an action, say, lying, is not inherently good or bad. The ethical significance of a lie depends on the effect it will have. If a lie could save someone's life, the lie could be ethically justified.

Deontology was the next ethical theory I shared with clients. In some ways, deontology is the opposite of consequentialism. From a deontological perspective, some actions are inherently good or bad, and no consequence would justify the bad actions. A deontologist might hold that deliberately taking a human life is always unethical, and that there is no justification for it, even saving another person's life.[9] I offered deontology to clients because it presents action guides in the form of rules, and we all are familiar with applying rules in some aspect of our lives. The next theory I shared was character-based ethics, sometimes called virtue ethics.[10] In contrast to deontology and consequentialism, character-based ethics focuses on developing virtues such as wisdom, courage, patience, and humility. While most of us are familiar with the idea of developing good character, the idea that developing character specifically aids in addressing dilemmas was new for many of my clients. From the perspective of character-based ethics, when we develop virtues, they will act as action guides in response to specific dilemmas, without our having to follow specific rules or use specific formulas, such as utilitarianism.

A fourth theory I shared with clients is often called rights-based ethical theory. Like consequentialism, many people are familiar with this theory, as it is embedded in much current political thought. From the perspective of rights-based ethical theory, we each have certain individual rights, such as a right not to be harmed, simply by virtue of being persons. The ways individuals interact with one another must respect these rights.[11] There is overlap between rights-based and deontological ethics, as rights often impose duties on us, such as a duty not to harm others, and rights and duties are often expressed as rules. In contrast, a rights-based approach to making a decision is in tension with a utilitarian approach to making a decision. Achieving the greatest good for the greatest number could infringe on a specific individual's rights, while attending to every individual's rights, in a given situation, could make achieving the greatest good for the greatest number impossible.

Communitarian ethical theory was the fifth type I shared with clients. Communitarian ethics prioritizes the common good, and often emphasizes the importance of values and traditions shared by a specific community as guides for action.[12] Clients found communitarianism relevant because, like all of us, each inhabited one or more communities: the organizations in which they worked; neighborhoods in which they lived; immediate and extended families; clubs and religious organizations to which they belonged. With a focus on the common good, a communitarian approach to making a decision can overlap with a utilitarian approach (although the greatest good for the greatest number may be different from the common good). Likewise, with its emphasis on having a community's values and traditions serve as action guides, communitarianism can overlap with character-based ethics.

The final type I shared with my clients was care-based ethical theory. According to this theory, care refers to concern for, emotional commitment to, and willingness to act on behalf of others to promote their well-being.[13] The care-based perspective emphasizes the interconnectedness of individuals and the impact of relationships on decision making. Clients found this theory relevant because they, again like all of us, exist in a web of relationships, and their dilemmas often involved how to maintain or strengthen relationships while pursuing other goals and priorities.

As I shared these theories over the course of multiple conversations, and supported my clients' deliberations, a method emerged. I observed clients combining all six theories into a process of ethical reasoning, to analyze and ultimately resolve dilemmas. The method involves asking questions about a dilemma from the perspective of each theory. Such questions include:

- What rules may be relevant to this dilemma? (*Deontological perspective*)
- What is the consequence I hope to see resulting from my decision? (*Consequentialist perspective*)
- What virtues (patience, courage, humility, etc.) are relevant to my choice, and what virtues do I want to develop and model through my choice? (*Character-based perspective*)
- What rights do the parties involved in the dilemma have, which must be respected? What rights do I have that must be respected? (*Rights-based perspective*)
- What community values and traditions should my choice reflect or embody? (*Communitarian perspective*)
- How will each possible course action affect the relationships of those involved in the dilemmas? What will build trust and fidelity and what would erode these? (*Care-based perspective*)

Clients also observed that they tended to prefer one or two theories to the others. For example, Simon observed that he most frequently used deontology in his day-to-day decision making, while Aviva observed she tended to be more consequentialist, and Matt found he tended to use rights-based theory most often. In some sense, learning ethical theory provided clients a vocabulary and framework to describe ways they were already approaching decisions. This did not surprise me. Although most people do not formally study ethical theory, ethical theories are embedded in many of our formative experiences, such as our family lives as children, and our educational, professional, civic, and religious experiences. We practice ethical theories without realizing we are doing so.

Because clients were aware that they preferred one or two types of theory to the others, deliberately taking themselves through the entire series of question became important as a means of ensuring they were examining their dilemmas thoroughly, rather than from those perspectives with which they were most familiar and comfortable.

Applying the various theories to their dilemmas also required Simon, Aviva, Varsha, Matt, and others to think abstractly and imaginatively. They often had to reason by analogy to recognize how a particular theory was relevant, or not so relevant, to their dilemma. For instance, Varsha stepped back from her dilemma and recognized it was a case of fair distribution of goods, and that the criteria she was using to distribute the goods – who is high potential vs. who has the longer tenure – were not adequate to determine a fair distribution of the MBA scholarships. In other words, the process of ethical reasoning I developed with my clients involved the cognitive ability to see the forest and the trees simultaneously. Clients needed to recognize what general categories a specific situation fits into, and they also needed the ability to recognize what was unique about a specific situation, so that they could adapt general principles into particular action guides for decision making.

To apply various ethical theories to their dilemmas, my clients also exercised ethical imagination, looking at their dilemmas from the perspectives of other people involved and mentally simulating how different courses of action could impact those people.[14] For example, Simon exercised ethical imagination by considering his career choice from his spouse's perspective, and Aviva exercised ethical imagination by looking at her decision from both her treasurer and member's perspective.

Revisiting Client Dilemmas

When Simon examined his dilemma – to stay in public health research or pursue a career in the pharmaceutical industry – using all six types of ethical theory, he found consequentialism, deontology, and character ethics to be the most illuminating. Applying consequentialism, Simon considered which career path would produce the greatest good for the greatest number of people. He concluded that pursuing a career in public health was more likely to produce the greatest good for the greatest number compared with a career in private industry. He came to the same conclusion applying deontology. A specific version of deontology, articulated by the eighteenth-century German philosopher Immanuel Kant, posits that every action should be generalizable.[15] In other words, before you take an action, you should ask yourself "Could every other person in this same situation take the exact action I am about to take?" Simon applied this question to himself, and concluded that if every researcher opted to leave public health for private industry, many diseases would go underresearched and potentially uncured. He found that his transition to private industry would not be generalizable to every person in his situation, so he concluded he should stay in public health. That Simon came to the same conclusion applying both deontology and consequentialism is interesting.

In theory, consequentialism and deontology can be opposed. If, for instance, as a deontologist you believe you have a duty never to harm, you would not justify causing harm in any circumstance, even if causing harm could result in a generally more positive outcome for more people. I have found through my years of work with clients that sharp distinctions between theories do not bear out in the practice of resolving dilemmas. As Simon illustrates, you can examine a dilemma from a number of theoretical positions and come to the same conclusion (which is actually helpful in zeroing in on what path you should pursue).

Finally, Simon considered his dilemma from the perspective of character ethics. He thought about how he wanted to develop his own character, as well as the character he wanted to model for others (younger researchers, possibly his own children). He concluded that for him to develop the kind of character he wanted to model for others, which included compassion, justice, conscientiousness, and integrity, he should stay in public health research. Considering his dilemma from the perspective of care-based ethics highlighted for Simon that he needed to involve his spouse in his deliberations, and keep in mind the impact his decision would have on their relationship. In fact, he discussed with his spouse the ways he was applying the ethical theories to their situation. By applying the theories in conversation together, they were able to agree mutually that Simon's pursuing a public health career was the better choice for them both.

When Aviva applied ethical theories to her dilemma – her fiduciary duty to her organization and her support for a refugee resettlement program that was outgrowing her organization – she found deontology and communitarianism most illuminating. Applying deontology clarified for Aviva that protecting the organization (limiting its exposure to liability; not burning out her treasurer) was her primary duty. Likewise, by assessing her dilemma from a communitarian perspective, she realized that her priority should be upholding and protecting the values of the entire community (and she should be serving as an example of the community's values).

She decided her organization could no longer administratively support the refugee resettlement program. Although the member who was instrumental in growing the resettlement program ended his membership with the organization, Aviva helped him establish his own 501c3 (a private, non-profit organization that is exempt from taxation) to support the growing resettlement initiative, and Aviva was one of his first board members.

When Varsha applied the different ethical theories to her dilemma – whether to fund one extremely high-potential employee to pursue an Ivy Leage MBA or three employees to pursue executive MBAs at a local state school – she found consequentialism and communitarianism most illuminating. By considering how to achieve the greatest good for the greatest number, Varsha concluded she could not fund only one employee to pursue a very expensive MBA, no matter how talented they were. Likewise, considering her dilemma from a communitarian perspective, Varsha realized privileging one individual with a degree at the expense of three other employees did not embody her organization's values. Varsha decided to offer the employee accepted to the Ivy League program tuition assistance (in the amount equivalent to full tuition at the local university), and also fully fund two additional employees pursuing executive MBAs locally. This solution allowed her to recognize the high potential of the one employee seeking the Ivy League degree, and to reward the loyalty of the two longer-term employees accepted to the local program. The high-potential employee gladly accepted the offer, and remained with the organization several years after completing her MBA.

Finally, Matt found deontology and care-based ethical theory the most illuminating of the theories, when he applied them to his personal dilemma – pursuing his dream promotion to the C-suite or continuing his parenting and caretaking roles. In a way similar to Simon, Matt specifically used the categorical imperative to analyze this dilemma. Also, like Simon, Matt concluded that a decision to pursue the C-suite promotion would not be generalizable. If everyone pursued a promotion at the expense of parenting and caretaking duties, there would be an extremely negative impact on family life and the fabric of society. Applying the care-based perspective, Matt also concluded that maintaining his relationship with his father, and strengthening his relationship with his soon-to-be adult children was more important than the promotion. Thus, Matt decided to forego the promotion. Ultimately, once his children were in college and his father passed away, Matt successfully sought a C-suite position in a different organization.

In subsequent conversations, I found that Simon, Aviva, Varsha, and Matt each felt they made the right choice. They reported feeling satisfied with their decisions, experiencing little to no regret, and experiencing increased self-confidence in their ability to resolve dilemmas going forward. When I explored these self-impressions with them, they each articulated that applying ethical theories helped them justify their decisions to themselves, and to other people. This ability to justify their decisions contributed to their satisfaction, reduced self-doubt, and increased self-esteem. While the idea of justifying decisions may sound legalistic, the ability to explain to yourself how a particular decision enacts your own values is psychologically, and ethically, important. Justification is demonstrating how a specific choice is right by furnishing adequate grounds for it.[16] The ethical reasoning methods my clients evolved as they examined their dilemmas through various ethical theories provided them these grounds and reasons for their decisions. They were able to explain to themselves how their choices deliberately enacted a specific ethical framework. Just as, if not more importantly, they were able to explain their decision-making processes to other people, which, in itself, was important for maintaining and strengthening their relationships.

A philosophical term for what Simon, Aviva, Varsha, Matt, and others achieved by applying different ethical theories to their dilemmas is reflective equilibrium. Reflective equilibrium is the balance between any pre-deliberative (intuitive) judgments you may have about a dilemma, your values, and the post-deliberative criteria you ultimately use to make a specific decision.[17] In other words, clients' efforts to refine their personal judgment evolved into a method of ethical reasoning, using analogies, imagination, and empathy to apply various ethical theories to a particular dilemma. Refining personal judgment and developing ethical reasoning allowed clients to resolve their dilemmas in ways that accorded with their own values and thus brought them a sense of satisfaction and well-being – a sense of having done the right thing to the best of their abilities.

Toolkit for Refining Your Personal Judgment

As discussed in Simon, Aviva, Varsha, and Matt's stories, a key way to refine your personal judgment is to practice ethical reasoning, which involves understanding and applying different ethical theories. To apply theories effectively, it is helpful to recognize which theories you currently apply to your decisions most frequently and least frequently. To get a snapshot of which ethical theories you currently use most and least when you face a dilemma, complete the questionnaire below.

Ethical Theories Questionnaire

For each prompt, put an "X" in the box – Usually, Sometimes, Seldom – that best describes the frequency with which you employ each theory.

Consequentialism

When I face a dilemma, I ...	Usually	Sometimes	Seldom
Think about how to achieve the greatest amount of good for the most people.			
Identify the outcome I want, then consider how to get there.			
Believe the end justifies the means in some cases.			

Deontology

When I face a dilemma, I ...	Usually	Sometimes	Seldom
Ask what obligations I have to other people.			
Ensure I am treating others as irreducibility valuable, not only as means to my ends.			
Ask if the action I'm about to take could be generalized into a universal rule applicable to everyone in a similar situation.			

Character-Based

When I face a dilemma, I ...	Usually	Sometimes	Seldom
Consider what character traits the situation calls for, such as courage or patience.			
Anticipate how a particular course of action could help or hurt my character.			
Consider how a particular course of action could affect the character development of others involved in the situation.			

Care-Based

When I face a dilemma, I ...	Usually	Sometimes	Seldom
Consider how pursuing a particular course of action will help or hurt my relationships with others involved in the situation.			
Ask if I need to put another person or group's needs ahead of my own.			
Ask if there is someone vulnerable or dependent in the situation whose interests I need to protect on their behalf.			

Rights-Based

When I face a dilemma, I . . .	Usually	Sometimes	Seldom
Identify what rights I have in the situation, such as a right to my own happiness.			
Ask if my exerting my rights is infringing on the rights of others involved in the situation.			
Consider if another party involved in the situation has rights that trump mine.			

Communitarian

When I face a dilemma, I ...	Usually	Sometimes	Seldom
Consider the way in which my action will reflect on a community of which I am a part (will it make others proud or ashamed of me).			
Recognize communal traditions I should uphold through my actions.			
Ask how my particular action promotes the common good.			

Note where you answered "Always" and "Sometimes." Do you see a pattern in your markings? If you see that you answered "Always" or "Sometimes" in response to all three items associated with a specific theory, your answers suggest you have a strong preference for that theory and that you may routinely use it in day-to-day decision making. Did you answer "Sometimes" or "Seldom" in response to the three items associated with a different theory? Your answers suggest you have a lower preference for this type of theory and may not use it frequently when you make decisions. Perhaps you do not see a pattern in your answers. If you do not see a pattern, do not worry. As discussed in the chapter, we are exposed to these theories without realizing it. We learn them at home, in school, and through participation in cultural, religious, and civic activities. Thus, everyone has the capacity to analyze a dilemma using all six theories, and to employ the ethical reasoning method I developed with my clients. Your responses to the questions above can give insights into the thought processes you bring to your dilemmas, as well as insights about theories you may benefit from applying more deliberately.

Practice Case Studies

Now that you have a sense of the ethical theories you apply most and least often, and a sense of how the theories form a method for approaching dilemmas, practice thinking from the perspective of each theory by applying them to the following four cases. This activity will reinforce your understanding of the theories as well as allow you to practice reasoning by analogy and using your ethical imagination. Assess each personal dilemma using these ethical reasoning questions:

- What duties and obligations may be relevant to this dilemma?
- What consequences ideally would result from resolving this dilemma?
- What virtues (patience, courage, humility, etc.) are relevant to this dilemma or could be developed in resolving this dilemma?
- What rights do the parties involved in the dilemma have, which must be respected?
- What community values and traditions could be relevant to this dilemma?
- How could each possible course action affect the relationships of those involved in the dilemma?

Personal Dilemma 1

Madison is in her mid-thirties, a single parent of two elementary school children. The public schools in Madison's area are not the strongest in terms of student test scores and college placements. Both of Madison's children are very intelligent and both have won scholarships to a local private K-12 school (kindergarten through 12th grade in the US) with an excellent reputation. Even with the scholarships, Madison pays $5,000 out-of-pocket for each child (full tuition for each child would be considerably more). Madison can afford the tuition, as well as buying her house and paying all other essential bills on her current salary. However, Madison feels she is stuck in a dead-end job, with little chance for advancement. Madison dreams of starting her own health and nutrition business, and has gained a lot of business acumen working as a manager for her current employer. She learns that a commercial space has become available near her house, which would be perfect for her dream business. Madison has saved money that she can use to start her business. Likewise, Madison's parents have offered to loan her money for startup costs. Madison would love to realize her dream of self-employment in the wellness industry, which ultimately could be much more lucrative than being an employee. Yet pursuing this dream would expose her and her family to financial volatility. Madison foresees not having the money to continue sending her children to better schools.

Dilemma Assessment Questions

- Analyze Madison's dilemma using the ethical reasoning questions representing the six types of ethical theory.
- How would you guide Madison in making this decision?
- Which theories seem most relevant and to provide the most clarity in Madison's situation?

Personal Dilemma 2

Nikkal is the executive director of a think tank. The think tank's mission is to produce non-partisan demographic, economic, energy, and survey research for use by state and local governments. Nikkal manages an interdisciplinary team of researchers, as well as an administrative staff of development, fiscal, and marketing personnel. The think tank is funded by government grants, corporate contributions, and individual donations. Recently, government funding has dropped. However, several individual donors have come forward and their contributions would more than compensate for the reduction in government grants. There is a condition: the new donors want a direct say regarding the issues the think tank researches and they want to review any findings and white papers before they are published. The think tank's board is divided. Half of the board members have advised Nikkal to turn down the donations, while the other half have advised him to accept them. Board members in both camps have threatened to resign if Nikkal does not follow their recommendations. Likewise, several senior researchers, who got wind of the donors' request, have threatened to leave for other think tanks, if Nikkal agrees to the donor's requests. Without additional funding soon, Nikkal may need to cut several positions, including a senior research position.

Dilemma Assessment Questions

- Analyze Nikkal's dilemma using the ethical reasoning questions representing the six types of ethical theory.
- How would you guide Nikkal in making this decision?
- Which theories seem most relevant and to provide the most clarity in Nikkal's situation?

Personal Dilemma 3

Aaron leads an organization that resettles refugee children in the United States. When the children arrive, after being flown to the United States by the Department of State, they stay for a few weeks in group facilities managed and maintained by Aaron's organization. Each facility is staffed by a psychologist, a food service provider, and four resident assistants who live on-site and provide 24-hour supervision and support to the children. Since the 2020 pandemic, hiring qualified child psychologists has become increasingly difficult. Aaron must offer higher salaries and better benefits to compete with other institutions. However, recruiting qualified resident assistants can also be a challenge. The role can be very demanding, and turnover is high. Aaron has found that higher pay and the promise of continuing education and certifications are both effective means to secure and retain qualified candidates for resident assistants. To compensate both psychologists and resident assistants at a higher level, Aaron has spent less on facilities maintenance and on food. This approach is proving problematic. Several facilities are now facing housing code infractions and one facility was recently cited by the local social services department for failing to meet nutritional requirements for the children. Aaron feels he is faced with cutting back on crucial services better to address facilities and food costs.

Dilemma Assessment Questions

- Analyze Aaron's dilemma using the ethical reasoning questions representing the six types of ethical theory.

- How would you guide Aaron in making this decision?
- Which theories seem most relevant and to provide the most clarity in Aaron's situation?

Personal Dilemma 4

Amy and her spouse, Quinn, have just purchased a house. They have been living in the same area for six years. Both have professional degrees. Amy is in private practice and Quinn works for a large research institution. They have two children, one in kindergarten and one in second grade. They live near Amy's aging parents and also near Amy's sister, who has mental health issues and is sporadically unemployed. Although Amy and Quinn have been pursuing a life-plan they agreed upon before getting married, Quinn has increasingly expressed frustration with the way their life is coming together. Quinn would like to live in a different geographical area, with a more temperate climate, a more diverse population, and a more progressive culture. Quinn has never felt at ease in their current area, and has become increasingly depressed and somewhat detached from their home life. With Amy's consent, Quinn applied for a position in a geographical area Quinn would prefer. Both Amy and Quinn felt the application would be a long shot. To their surprise, Quinn has been offered the position. In addition to being in Quinn's preferred area, the position is at a more prestigious institution than Quinn's current role, and it offers a greater chance of advancement. The new position pays more, although the new region is more expensive than where Quinn and Amy currently live. Quinn is ecstatic and wants to take the position and relocate the family. Amy agreed for Quinn to apply mainly as a goodwill gesture, and never imagined Quinn would be offered the job. Now Amy is worried about how to re-establish her practice in a new area. She is also concerned about uprooting their children, possibly losing money on selling their house, and leaving her parents and sister. Quinn's new position is a four-hour flight from where Quinn and Amy currently live. Amy is not sure she wants to move, or that Quinn should accept the new position.

Dilemma Assessment Questions

- Do you think this situation represents a dilemma for both Amy and Quinn, or only one of them?
- Analyze the situation using the ethical reasoning questions representing the six types of ethical theory.
- Which theories seem most relevant and to provide the most clarity for the situation?
- How would you guide both Amy and Quinn?

Progress Journal

Progress Journal – Week 1

Weekly Self-Reflection

- What dilemmas did you encounter this week (work-related, personal, other)?
- How did you apply ethical reasoning to the dilemma?
- What questions did you ask to contextualize and better understand the dilemma?
- What insights did you gain by applying your personal judgment to the dilemma?

Pulse-Check

0	1	2	3	4	5	6	7	8	9	10
Not at all			Somewhat					Absolutely		

Using the scale given above, rate your degree of confidence below by recording a number from 0 to 10 in the column on the right.

Please rate how confident you are that you can:

Recognize situations that are dilemmas	
Apply ethical reasoning to analyze a dilemma	
Apply your personal judgment to a dilemma	
Resolve a dilemma in a way that aligns with your values and aspirations	

Progress Journal – Week 2

Weekly Self-Reflection

- What dilemmas did you encounter this week (work-related, personal, other)?
- How did you apply ethical reasoning to the dilemma?
- What questions did you ask to contextualize and better understand the dilemma?
- What insights did you gain by applying your personal judgment to the dilemma?

Pulse-Check

0	1	2	3	4	5	6	7	8	9	10
Not at all			Somewhat					Absolutely		

Using the scale given above, rate your degree of confidence below by recording a number from 0 to 10 in the column on the right.

Please rate how confident you are that you can:

Recognize situations that are dilemmas	
Apply ethical reasoning to analyze a dilemma	
Apply your personal judgment to a dilemma	
Resolve a dilemma in a way that aligns with your values and aspirations	

Progress Journal – Week 3

Weekly Self-Reflection

- What dilemmas did you encounter this week (work-related, personal, other)?
- How did you apply ethical reasoning to the dilemma?
- What questions did you ask to contextualize and better understand the dilemma?
- What insights did you gain by applying your personal judgment to the dilemma?

Pulse-Check

0	1	2	3	4	5	6	7	8	9	10
Not at all					Somewhat					Absolutely

Using the scale given above, rate your degree of confidence below by recording a number from 0 to 10 in the column on the right.

Please rate how confident you are that you can:

Recognize situations that are dilemmas	
Apply ethical reasoning to analyze a dilemma	
Apply your personal judgment to a dilemma	
Resolve a dilemma in a way that aligns with your values and aspirations	

Progress Journal – Week 4

Final Self-Reflection and Assessment

- How has your approach to resolving dilemmas changed in the past four weeks?
- How has your self-perception of your decision making changed in the past four weeks?
- What are two to three situations in which you feel you used your personal judgment effectively to solve a problem or make a decision?
- Describe a situation in which you could have used your personal judgment more effectively. What would you do differently?
- What skills or habits of mind do you need to enhance going forward?
- What resources and support do you need to continue to develop skills?

Notes

1 For a more detailed version of this case, see Tom L. Beauchamp and James F. Childress, *Principles of Biomedical Ethics* (Oxford University Press, 2019), 49.

2 My description of deliberation in informed by the American twentieth-century philosopher John Dewey's account in *Theory of the Moral Life* (Holt, Reinhardt and Winston, 1960).

3 For a useful discussion of the reasons people consult advice columns, see Elizabeth Wolfe, "Words from a Failed Advice Columnist," *The Michigan Daily*, March 28, 2023.

4 Rushworth Kidder, *How Good People Make Tough Choices* (Harper Perennial, 2009).

5 Emalyn Opido, "The Three Levels of Moral Dilemmas," *Scribed*, https://www.scribd.com/document/445213147/The-Three-Level-of-Moral-Dilemmas-docx.

6 Aviva was referring to the social intuitionist model developed social psychologist Jonathan Haidt. Articulated in his 2001 paper "The Emotional Dog and its Rational Tail: A Social Intuitionist Approach to Moral Judgments," the model asserts that moral reasoning often serves as a post hoc justification for already formed intuitions. See Jonathan Haidt, *Psychological Review* 108, no. 4 (2001): 814–834.

7 Aviva was referring to Jonathan Haidt's theory of moral foundations and its use of evolutionary psychology. Haidt proposes that humans have five moral foundations, which have developed through humans' evolution, as means to address challenges in the prehistoric environment. The foundations are: care/harm; fairness/cheating, loyalty/betrayal; authority/subversion; sanctity/degradation; liberty/oppression. See Jonathan Haidt, *The Righteous Mind: Why Good People are Divided by Politics and Religion* (Penguin Random House, 2013). Haidt's theory is similar to the theory of moral sentiments proposed by the eighteenth-century Scottish philosopher and economist Adam Smith. See Adam Smith, *Theory of Moral Sentiments* (Penguin Classics, 2010). It is not clear that Haidt's theory of moral foundations must necessarily be connected with the claims of evolutionary psychology. There could be other origins of the foundations. See Chapter 4 of this book for a more detailed discussion of evolutionary psychology.

8 The most well-known version of consequentialism is utilitarianism, first articulated by the eighteenth-century British philosopher Jeremy Bentham. See Jeremy Bentham, *The Principles of Morals and Legislation* (Oxford University Press, 1996), and given fuller exposition by mid-nineteenth-century British philosopher John Stewart Mill in *Utilitarianism* (Hackett Publishing, 2002).

9 The most prominent account of deontology is the work of eighteenth-century German philosopher Immanuel Kant. See Immanuel Kant, *Metaphysics of Morals* (Cambridge University Press, 2017).

10 While Aristotle presented a version of character ethics, the best-known contemporary articulation is that of Alasdair McIntyre, *After Virtue: A Study in Moral Theory* (University of Notre Dame Press, 1981).

11 For an overview of rights-based ethics, see Ronald Dworkin, *Taking Rights Seriously* (Harvard University Press, 1977).

12 For an overview of communitarian ethics, see Michael Sandel, *Liberalism and the Limits of Justice* (New York University Press, 1984).

13 The best-known proponent of care-based ethics may be Carol Gilligan, *In a Different Voice* (Harvard University Press, 1982).

14 Adam Smith introduced the concept of ethical imagination in his *Theory of Moral Sentiments*. For a contemporary discussion of ethical imagination, see Patricia H. Werhane, *Moral Imagination and Management Decision Making* (Oxford University Press, 1999).

15 Immanuel Kant, *Metaphysics of Morals* (Cambridge University Press, 2017).

16 Tom L. Beauchamp and James F. Childress, *Principles of Biomedical Ethics* (Oxford University Press, 2019), 13.

17 Although American philosopher Nelson Goodman, mentioned in Chapter 3, first described the components of reflective equilibrium in *Fact, Fiction, Forecast* (Harvard University Press, 1983), the later American philosopher John Rawls introduced the term "reflective equilibrium" in *A Theory of Justice* (Harvard University Press, 1999).

Bibliography and Additional Reading

American Psychological Association. "Cognitive Psychology." *Dictionary of Psychology.* Last updated April 4, 2019. https://dictionary.apa.org/cognitive-psychology.

Aragones, Enriqueta, Itzhak Gilboa, Andrew Postlewaite, and David Schmeidler. "From Cases to Rules: Induction and Regression." University of Pennsylvania School of Arts and Sciences, April, 2002. https://www.sas.upenn.edu/~apostlew/paper/pdf/AGPS_From_Cases_to_Rules.pdf.

Ariely, Dan. *The Upside of Irrationality: The Unexpected Benefits of Defying Logic.* Harper-Collins, 2011.

Aristotle. *Nicomachean Ethics,* edited by Robert Williams. Oxford University Press, 1998.

Aristotle. *Rhetoric,* edited by Edward Meredith Cope and John Edwin Sandys. Cambridge University Press, 2010.

Armstrong, J. Scott. "Evaluating Forecasting Methods." In *Principles of Forecasting: A Handbook for Researchers and Practitioners,* edited by J. Scott Armstrong. Kluwer Academic Publishers, 2001.

Bailey, Drew H., Alexander J. Jung, Adriene M. Beltz, et al. "Causal Inference on Human Behavior." *Nature Human Behavior* 8, no. 8 (August, 2024): 1448–1459.

Bandura, Alfred. *Self-Efficacy: The Exercise of Control.* Worth Publishers, 1997.

Bardach, Eugene. *A Practical Guide for Policy Analysis: The Eightfold Path to More Effective Problem Solving.* CQ Publishing, 2005.

Beauchamp, Tom L. and James F. Childress. *Principles of Biomedical Ethics.* Oxford University Press, 2019.

Bellah, Robert N., Richard Madsen, William Sullivan, et al. *Habits of the Heart: Individualism and Commitment in American Life.* Harper & Row Publishers, 1985.

Bentham, Jeremy. *The Principles of Moral and Legislation.* Oxford University Press, 1996.

Berger, Peter L. and Thomas Luckman. *The Social Construction of Reality: A Treatise in the Sociology of Knowledge.* Anchor Books, 1966.

Black, Max. "Induction." *The Encyclopedia of Philosophy,* edited by Paul Edwards. Macmillan and The Free Press, 1967.

Bradley, F. H. *Essays on Truth and Reality.* Cambridge University Press, 2011.

Bryan, Christopher J., Elizabeth Tipton, and David S. Yeager. "Behavioural Science Is Unlikely to Change the World Without a Heterogeneity Revolution." *Nature Human Behavior* 5, no. 8 (August, 2021): 981–989.

Budak, C., Nyhan, B., Rothschild, D. M., et al. "Misunderstanding the Harms of Online Misinformation." *Nature* 630 (2024).

Canadian Securities Institute website. "Study Tools." Accessed January, 2025. https://www.csi.ca/en/learning/courses/csc/study-tools.

Carlyle, Thomas. *Hero-Worship and the Heroic in History*, edited by Michael Goldberg. University of California Press, 1993.

Caulfield, Mike and Sam Wineburg. *Verified: How to Think Straight, Get Duped Less, And Make Better Decisions About What to Believe Online*. University of Chicago Press, 2023.

Cefkin, Melissa, ed. *Ethnography and the Corporate Encounter: Reflections on Research in and of the Corporation*. Berghahn Books, 2009.

Chamber, John C., Satinder K. Mullik, and Donald D. Smith, "How to Choose the Right Forecasting Technique." *Harvard Business Review*, 1971.

Chartrand, Judy, Stewart Emery, Russ Hall, et al. *Now You Are Thinking: Change Your Thinking, Transform Your Life*. Pearson Education, 2012.

Chase, Richard B. and Sriram Dasu. "Want to Perfect Your Company's Service? Use Behavioral Science." *Harvard Business Review*, June, 2001.

Chrisley, Ron. "A Human-Centered Approach to AI Ethics: A Perspective from Cognitive Science." In *The Oxford Handbook of Ethics of AI*, edited by Marcus D. Dubber, Frank Pasquale, and Sunit Das. Oxford University Press, 2020.

Cicero. *On Oratory and Orators*, edited and translated by J. S. Watson. Southern Illinois University Press, 1986.

Clayton, Aubrey. *Bernoulli's Fallacy: Statistical Illogic and the Crisis of Modern Science*. Cambridge University Press, 2021.

Coyne, Anthony M. *Introduction to Inductive Reasoning*. University Press of America, 1984.

Davidson, Donald, Patrick Suppes, and Sidney Siegel. *Decision-Making: An Experimental Approach*. Praeger, 1977.

Deroover, Kristine, Simon Knight, and Tamara Bucher. "Why Do Experts Disagree? The Development of a Taxonomy." *Public Understanding of Science* 32, no. 2 (August 1, 2022): 224–246.

Dewey, John. *Theory of the Moral Life*. Holt, Reinhardt and Winston, 1960.

Djerf-Pierre, M. and Ekström, M. "Constructive Journalism as Practice – Storytelling in Solutions-Focused News Reporting in Mainstream News Media." *Journalism Practice* (2025): 1–19.

Donaldson, Thomas, Patricia Werhane, and Margaret Cording. *Ethical Issues in Business*. Pearson College Division, 7th edition, 2002.

Drazen, Allan, Anna Dreber, Eric Snowberg, et al. "Journal-Based Replication of Experiments." *Journal of Public Economics*, 202 (October, 2021): 401–482.

Durkheim, Emile. *The Rules of Sociological Method and Selected Texts on Sociology*, edited by Steven Lukes, translated by W. D. Hall. The Free Press, 1982.

Dworkin, Ronald. *Taking Rights Seriously*. Harvard University Press, 1977.

Evans, Jonathan, St. B. T. *Hypothetical Thinking: Dual Process in Reasoning and Judgment*. Psychology Press, 2007.

Fischhoff, Baruch. "What Forecasts (Seem to) Mean." *International Journal of Forecasting* 10, no. 3 (1994): 387–403.

Freddie Mac House Price Index Price Appreciation 1990–2023. Statista.com. https://www.statista.com/statistics/275159/freddie-mac-house-price-index-from-2009/.

Galo, Amy. "A Refresher on Regression Analysis." *Harvard Business Review*, November 4, 2015.

Gannon, Megan. "Race is a Social Construct, Scientists Argue." *Scientific American*, February 6, 2016. https://www.scientificamerican.com/article/race-is-a-social-construct-scientists-argue/.

Gilligan, Carol. *In a Different Voice*. Harvard University Press, 1982.

Gladwell, Malcolm. *Blink: The Power of Thinking Without Thinking*. Little, Brown, 2005.

Goodman, Nelson. *Fact, Fiction Forecast*. Harvard University Press, 1983.

Gordon, Michael, Domenico Viganola, Anna Dreber, et al. "Predicting Replicability: Analysis of Survey and Prediction Market Data from Large-Scale Forecasting Projects." *PLOS ONE* 16, no. 4 (April, 2021). https://pmc.ncbi.nlm.nih.gov/articles/PMC8046229/.

Grant, Adam. *Originals: How Non-Conformists Move the World*. Penguin, 2017.

Grosz, Michael P., Julia M. Rohrer, and Felix Thoemmes. "The Taboo Against Explicit Causal Inference in Nonexperimental Psychology." *Perspectives on Psychology* 15, no. 5 (July, 2020): 1243–1255.

Hacking, Ian. *The Social Construction of What?* Harvard University Press, 1999.

Haidt, Jonathan. "The Emotional Dog and its Rational Tail: A Social Intuitionist Approach to Moral Judgments." *Psychological Review* 108, no. 4 (2001): 814–834.

Haidt, Jonathan. *The Righteous Mind: Why Good People are Divided by Politics and Religion*. Penguin Random House, 2013.

Halpern, Diane. *Thought and Knowledge: An Introduction to Critical Thinking*. Lawrence Erlbaum Associates, 1989.

Hannon, Michael. "Public Discourse and Its Problems." *Politics, Philosophy and Economics* 22, no. 3 (August, 2023): 336–365.

Hasso, Tim, Mark Brosnan, Daniel Chai, et al. "Perceived Problems, Causes, and Solutions of Finance Research and Replicability: A Pre-Registered Report." *Pacific-Basin Finance Journal* 91 (October 18, 2024): 1025–1064.

Haw, Rebecca, "Conflicting Expert Witnesses Can Give Inaccurate View of Science." Interviewed by Vanderbilt University School of Law. *Vanderbilt Research News*. https://news.vanderbilt.edu/2012/04/09/dueling-witnesses/.

Hayek, F. A. "The Pretense of Knowledge." *The American Economic Review* 9, no. 6 (December, 1989): 3–7. (Reprinted from original lecture given in 1974.)

Henriques, Greg. "The Metaphysical Mysteries of Life, Mind and Culture." *Psychology Today*, May 29, 2020.

Horgan, John. "Beyond the One and Only Truth." *Scientific American,* September 19, 2019. https://www.scientificamerican.com/blog/cross-check/pluralism-beyond-the-one-and-only-truth/.

Hume, David. *Enquiry Concerning Human Understanding*, edited by Eric Steinberg. Hackett, 1993.

Hume, David. *A Treatise of Human Nature*, edited by David Fate Norton and Mary J. Norton. Oxford University Press, 2000.

IJzerman, H., Lewis, N. A., Przybylski, A. K., et al. "Use Caution When Applying Behavioural Science to Policy." *Nature Human Behavior* 4 (2020): 1092–1094.

Ions, Edward. *Against Behaviouralism: A Critique of Behavioural Science*. Basil Blackwell, 1977.

James, William. *The Will to Believe*, edited by Frederick Burkhardt, Fredson Bowers, and Ignas K. Skrupskelis. Harvard University Press, 1979.

James, William. *Principles of Psychology*, Volumes 1–2. Harvard University Press, 1983.

James, William. *Pragmatism: A New Name for Some Old Ways of Thinking*. Meyers Education Press, 2019.

Jensen, Theis, Bryan Kelly, and Lasse Pedersen. "Is There a Replication Crisis in Finance." *The Journal of Finance* 78, no. 5 (May 26, 2023): 2465–2518.

Joachim, Harold. *The Nature of Truth*. The Clarendon Press, 1906.

Kahane, Howard. *Logic and Contemporary Rhetoric: The Use of Reasoning in Everyday Life*. University of Kansas Press, 2017.

Kahneman, Daniel and Amos Tversky. "Prospect Theory: An Analysis of Decision Under Risk." *Econometrica* 47, No. 2 (March, 1979): 263–291.

Kahneman, Daniel, Amos Tversky and Paul Slovic. *Judgement Under Uncertainty: Heuristics and Biases*. Cambridge University Press, 1982.

Kant, Immanuel. *Metaphysics of Morals*. Cambridge University Press, 2017.

Keysers, Christian, Valeria Gazzola, and Eric-Jan Wagonmakers. "Using Bayes Factor Hypothesis Testing in Neuroscience to Establish Evidence of Absence." *National Neuroscience* 23, no. 7 (June 29, 2020): 788–799. https://pubmed.ncbi.nlm.nih.gov/32601411/#:~:text=Abstract,the%20absence%20of%20an%20effect.

Kidder, Rushworth. *How Good People Make Tough Choices*. Harper Perennial, 2009.

Knobe, J. "Experimental Philosophy." *The Stanford Encyclopedia of Philosophy*. Updated December 19, 2017. https://plato.stanford.edu/entries/experimental-philosophy/.

Kolbert, Elizabeth. "What Was I Thinking: The Latest Reasoning About Our Irrational Ways." *The New Yorker*, February 25, 2008.

Korteling, Johan E., Anne-Marie Brouwer, and Alexander Toet, "A Neural Network Framework for Cognitive Bias." *Frontiers in Psychology* 9 (September 2, 2018). https://www.frontiersin.org/journals/psychology/articles/10.3389/fpsyg.2018.01561/full.

Lenz, Robert W. "Hume's Defense of Causal Inference." *Journal of the History of Ideas* 19, no. 4 (1958): 559–567.

Leslie, Julian C. "The Relevance of Metaphysics for Behavior Analysis." *Perspectives on Behavior Science* 44 (March, 2021): 29–40.

Loeb, Louis. "Inductive Inference in Hume's Philosophy." *A Companion to Hume*, edited by Elizabeth F. Radcliffe. Wiley, 2008.

Lynch, Michael. *Truth as One and Many*. Oxford University Press, 2009.

Mach, Ernst. *Popular Scientific Lectures*, translated by Thomas J. McCormack. Cambridge University Press, 2014.

Madsen, Jens Koed, Lee de Wit, Peter Ayton, et al. "Behavioral Science Should Start by Assuming People Are Reasonable." *Trends in Cognitive Science* 28, no. 7 (July, 2024): 583–585.

Mayo, Deborah G. *Statistical Inference as Severe Testing: How to Get Beyond the Statistics Wars*. Cambridge University Press, 2018.

McIntyre, Alasdair. *After Virtue: A Study in Moral Theory*. University of Notre Dame Press, 1981.

Meade, George Herbert. *Mind, Self and Society from the Standpoint of a Social Behaviorist*. University of Chicago Press, 1967.

Meszanos, John. "A Brief Review of House Price Forecasting Methods." *The Counselors of Real Estate* 48, no. 4 (February 7, 2024). https://cre.org.real-estate-issues/a-brief-review-of-house-price-forecasting-methods/.

Mill, John Stewart Mill. *Utilitarianism*. Hackett, 2002.

Neuberg, Leland Gerson. "Hume's Problem of Induction in Modern Statistical Inference and Controlled Experimentation." In *Conceptual Anomalies in Economics and Statistics*, edited by Leland Gerson Neuberg. Cambridge University Press, 2010.

Nickerson, Raymond S. *Teaching Reasoning*. Cambridge University Press, 2004.

Nozick, Robert. *The Nature of Rationality*. Princeton University Press, 1993.

"Nudge U." Blog. Harvard University. Accessed April, 2025. www.nudgeu.harvard.edu.

Opido, Emalyn. "The Three Levels of Moral Dilemmas." *Scribed*. https://www.scribd.com/document/445213147/The-Three-Level-of-Moral-Dilemmas-docx.

Optimizely.com. Accessed December, 2024. https://www.optimizely.com/optimizationglossary/behavioral-science/.

"Our Definition of the Scientific Method." The Science Council. Accessed April, 2025. https://sciencecouncil.org/about-science/our-definition-of-science/.

Pagani, Dean. "On Storytelling in Journalism." *Medium*, April 2, 2022. https://deanpagani.medium.com/on-story-telling-in-journalism-4edd7412c714.

Pareto, Vilfredo. *The Manual of Political Economy*, edited by Aldo Montesano. Oxford University Press, 2006.

Pedersen, Nikolaj and Cory Wright, eds. *Truth Pluralism: Current Debates*. Oxford University Press, 2012.

Pierce, Charles S. *Illustrations in the Logic of Science*, edited by Carnelis de Waal. Open Court Publishing, 2014.

Pierce, Charles S. *How to Make Our Ideas Clear: The Fixation of Our Belief*. LM Publishing, 2024.

Polman, Evan and Sam J. Maglio. "Will Your Nudge Have a Lasting Impact." *Harvard Business Review*, April 29, 2024.

Popper, Karl. *The Logic of Scientific Discovery*. Routledge. 2002.

Powers, Thomas M. and Jean-Gabriel Ganascia. "The Ethics of AI." *The Oxford Handbook of Ethics of AI*, edited by Marcus D. Dubber, Frank Pasquale, and Sunit Das. Oxford University Press, 2020.

Rawls, John. *A Theory of Justice*. Harvard University Press, 1999.

Reis-Dennis, S., M. S. Gerrity, and G. Geller. "Tolerance for Uncertainty and Professional Development: A Normative Analysis." *Journal of General Internal Medicine* 36 (2021): 2408–2413.

Reissman, Hailey. "What Public Discourse Gets Wrong About Misinformation Online." *Research News*. Annenberg School for Communication, University of Pennsylvania. https://www.asc.upenn.edu/news-events/news/what-public-discourse-gets-wrong-about-misinformation-online.

Ribeiro, Gustavo Sampaio A. "No Need to Toss a Coin: Conflicting Scientific Expert Testimonies and Intellectual Due Process." *Law, Probability and Risk* 12, no. 4 (September–December, 2013): 299–342.

Rodriguez, James. "Zillow's Price Estimates Are Screwing up Homebuying." *Yahoo Finance Business Insider*, December 18, 2024. https://www.msn.com/en/us/money/realestate/ar-AA1w4xFn.

Russell, Bertrand. *The Problems of Philosophy*. Oxford University Press, 13th edition, 1965.

Saffo, Paul. "Six Rules for Effective Forecasting." *Harvard Business Review*, July, 2007.

Sahay, Arun. *Sociological Analysis*. Routledge & Kegan Paul, 1972.

Sandel, Michael. *Liberalism and the Limits of Justice*. New York University Press, 1984.

Sandel, Michael. *Public Philosophy: Essays on Morality in Politics*. Harvard University Press, 2008.

Science Council. https://sciencecouncil.org/about-science/our-definition-of-science/.

Shermer, Michael. *The Believing Brain: From Ghosts and Gods to Politics and Conspiracies – How We Construct Beliefs and Reinforce Them as Truths*. Macmillan, 2011.

Smith, Adam. *The Theory of Moral Sentiments*. Penguin Classics, 2010.

Stephens, G. C. and M. D. Lazarus. "Twelve Tips for Developing Healthcare Learners' Uncertainty Tolerance." *Medical Teacher* 46, no. 8 (2024): 1035–1043.

Stobierski, Tim. "A Beginner's Guide to Hypothesis Testing." Harvard Business School, Business Insights Blog. March 30, 2021. https://online.hbs.edu/blog/post/hypothesis-testing.

"Storytelling and Characters in Broadcast Journalism." NBCU Academy. Updated April 3, 2024. https://nbcuacademy.com/storytelling-characters/.

Stove, David. "Hume, Probability and Induction." *The Philosophical Review* 74, no. 2 (1965): 399–430.

Strawson, Peter. *Individuals: An Essay in Descriptive Metaphysics*. Routledge, 1964.

Sunstein, Cass R. and Richard Thaler. *Nudge: Improving Decisions About Health, Wealth and Happiness*. Penguin, 2008.

Thaler, Richard H. "The Overconfidence Problem in Forecasting." *The New York Times*, August 21, 2010.

University of Chicago Booth School of Business, Mindworks Institute. https://www.chicagobooth.edu/mindworks/what-is-behavioral-science-research.

Wagenmakers, Eric-Jan, Michael Lee, Geoff Iverson, et al. "Bayesian Versus Frequentist Inference." *Bayesian Evaluation of Informative Hypothesis, Statistics for Social and Behavior Sciences*, edited by P. A. Boelen. Springer, 2008.

Walzer, Michael. *Spheres of Justice: A Defense of Pluralism and Equality*. Basic Books, 1983.

Warren, Robert Penn and Cleanth Brooks. *Modern Rhetoric*. Harcourt, Brace, Jovanovich, 1979.

Washington and Lee University, Department of Cognitive and Behavioral Science website. https://www.wlu.edu/academics/areas-of-study/cognitive-and-behavioral-science.

Werhane, Patricia H. *Moral Imagination and Management Decision Making*. Oxford University Press, 1999.

Whitehead, Alfred North. *Science and the Modern World*. The Free Press, 1997.

Wittgenstein, Ludwig. *On Certainty*. Edited by G. E. M. Anscomb and G. H. von Wright. Harper Perennial Modern Thought, 1972.

Wolfe, Elizabeth. "Words from a Failed Advice Columnist." *The Michigan Daily*, March 28, 2023.

Wright, Crispin. *Truth and Objectivity*. Harvard University Press, 1994.

Vandeveld, Kenneth J. *Thinking Like a Lawyer: An Introduction to Legal Reasoning*. Routledge, 2010.

Index

For Product Safety Concerns and Information please contact our EU
representative GPSR@taylorandfrancis.com
Taylor & Francis Verlag GmbH, Kaufingerstraße 24, 80331 München, Germany

www.ingramcontent.com/pod-product-compliance
Lightning Source LLC
Chambersburg PA
CBHW070348270326
41926CB00017B/4044